# Journey to Joy

*How to Overcome*
*Life's Setbacks to Create*
*a Life you Love*



**By Frances Hickmott**

HarBoy Books
Canada

Published by HarBoy Books, 2019



Library and Archives Canada
ISBN 978-1-9991993-0-2 Trade Paperback
ISBN 978-1-9991993-1-9 EPub

# TABLE OF CONTENTS

# Preface

The end of the world, apocalypse stories have long been told and for many are interesting because they fall in the realm of fiction. Through those stories we watch who people become when the normal world slips away. We follow the characters as they grapple with the internal and external forces and see how they choose to respond.

Those scenarios let us be spectators rather than participants and give us the luxury of relaxing as armchair adventurers, imagining how we might respond if the worst came to pass. But, for some of us, we are faced with those challenges early on and our normal is not the normal of those around us. In fact, the experiences may fall under the umbrella of trauma, even though we may never have identified it as such. I know I didn't.

This book is part memoir and part guide. As I began to grapple with some of the fallouts of my childhood experiences I learned to see with a new lens. To consider new possibilities and to begin to ask and answer the big questions like: "Who am I?" and "What matters?" and "Why am I here?"

But, when our life challenges emerge, we are thrown from spectator to a participant role. We may find ourselves re-thinking what we know of ourselves and the world, and yes, even asking those age-old questions.

I have included some stories of my own life but also from others kind enough to share parts of their experiences in creating a life of meaning and joy. In some cases, I have changed the names to protect the privacy of those who would rather not be identified. I am deeply grateful that they allowed me to share their stories.

I recall reading a researcher saying that essentially all research is “me-search” especially within the realm of psychology and behaviour. It was just that push that ultimately led to me to ask the big questions and to seek the help I needed to come fully into myself.

This book is not specifically about finding happiness, although you may find some ideas about becoming happier. Rather, the purpose of this book is to help those of you searching out the answers to those life questions. Not because I have all the answers, but rather because I have at different times, been challenged to ask them.

My hope is that this book will provide you with the knowledge of the universality of struggle and of transforming those experiences into lives of meaning.

Part 1 is Reality Check. Here I share how we can identify what isn’t working or satisfying in our life, and when finding ourselves at such a point, acknowledging the feelings that arise. It is that point, those uncomfortable feelings, that I invite you to explore, so that you may grow into a life of your intentional creation.

In addition to some of the lessons I have learned, you will also find research that sheds light on loneliness, mindset and happiness.

Part 2 is Reconciliation and Transformation and contains ideas and stories drawn from my own life and others, about how to create the life you want.

In my life and my work, I operate from two main principles. The first is that there is something to learn from everyone and the second is that the more I learn, the more I realize how little I know.

Because this is a book about "life," I cannot claim the title of expert. Really, like any of us, I am an apprentice. However, in the area of self-leadership, which is the basis of how any of us are truly able to create a life of meaning, I bring to you everything I have learned.

This is where I hope to ignite your thoughts and feelings about your potential to create the life you are seeking. We all carry stories from our past, but it is self-leadership that carries us forward. It is my sincere desire that this book adds to your knowledge and self-awareness so that you feel inspired as you travel your own journey to joy.

# Introduction

"Hurry up," he said. "It's time to go."

"I'm not ready."

He frowned.

I got into the passenger side of the car, and he got into the driver's side. The baby was in the back, but she wasn't yet fastened in. Before I could secure her or put my seat belt on, the car was backing up and taking off.

"Wait, wait!"

He was impervious to my pleas and shrieks. Suddenly, we were off the road. As I came to, the car was on its side in a ditch, and the driver and baby had disappeared. I was all alone, afraid, and didn't know what to do.

I awoke from the nightmare with the realization that for too long I'd been the passenger in my life. It was a true wake up call, a plea from the subconscious to get real and take charge.

The car was my life: much of it driven by other people's ideas, expectations, and opinions. The baby was—and remains—my dream of living a fulfilling life, one that uses my talents and gifts.

Taking the wheel means taking responsibility for your life. That's what self-leadership is: moving from passenger to driver.

Regardless of our backstory, gender or age, the greatest gift we can give to ourselves and the world is to become fully ourselves. To define our values, determine our vision for our lives, and use our talents and skills for ourselves and the world we live in.

Self-leadership is what helps us overcome life's trials and tribulations. It is resilience and connectedness, achievement, and happiness. If we are connected to who we are and the value we have as individuals, then it is possible for us to create and live the lives of meaning and purpose that we seek. The first and biggest decision is choosing to be the driver. The second is learning how to drive!

For those of you who are feeling foolish, scared, worried—or the thousand other things that might come up when you take this ginormous step—remember that every skill is something you've learned how to do or can learn to do. And importantly, remember you are not alone. Your friends, family and others you don't even know yet are awaiting your arrival on the other side!

This book is what I've learned about becoming the driver and how to find your way around even some of life's biggest obstacles. It's part motivation and part inspiration, with side orders of knowledge and a kick in the pants.

When you show up and live your life in a way that lets your light shine, it brightens up your corner of the world. Think of a field of fireflies: magical, beautiful, and inspiring. When you're living your life fully, expressing your whole self, it is equally magical, beautiful, and inspiring.

Ready? Let's do this because you deserve to be in the driver's seat!

# Part One: Reality Check

# Chapter 1: State of the Union – (Restless)

**"What lies behind us and what lies before us are tiny matters, compared to what lies within us."**

**Ralph Waldo Emerson**

Where does the first ripple of restlessness come from? One day you are coasting along and all seems well, and the next a feeling arrives, like a mosquito in the middle of the night that won't stop buzzing around your ears.
It is irritating. If you cannot find and squash it, the next thing you know, there is an itch you cannot get rid of. Getting that itch can lead to truly amazing things.

Just like a mosquito, restlessness can be uninvited and unexpected. Other times, like parenthood, we know it is imminent.

When we become parents, we jump in, and it is all consuming. Parenthood is a bit like contract work. There is definitely a start date, but unless there are specific circumstances that make your intense parenting ongoing, you're going to find yourself out of work.

There will always be some bit of you involved, but all things being equal, your kids will grow up, and then you'll have time to fill. And maybe, like me, some personal discovery to launch into.

I'd known the day would come, and I certainly planned to work myself out of the job. Yet as the reality stared me in the face, I realized I hadn't planned what to do once that job no longer existed.

Does that sound familiar? If not parenthood, perhaps the end of your academic studies, a caregiving role, a relationship or even your career. Life is a cycle of beginnings and endings. Regardless of what the ending is, you may find yourself with more time than you've had in years and no clear idea of what to do with it.

Especially if you've been using busyness and roles as the definitions of who you are. Take those away, and you're faced with an identity crisis. It's unsettling, worrisome.

Then you begin to ask the big questions. Who am I? Why am I here?

If these questions are frightening, you might find yourself looking for ways to ignore or push them down. Which works, until it doesn't.

Poet Anaïs Nin captures the feeling exquisitely:

And the day came when the risk to remain tight in a bud was more painful than the risk it took to blossom.

## My Story

My life has taken some twists and turns, some by choice and some by chance. One especially big twist was when my family and I took on the guardianship of my niece and nephew after the death of my sister. We went from two teenagers and one bathroom to four teenagers and one bathroom. Life changed, a lot. After an intense period of parenting I looked forward to more me time. I was still working as both an employee and as co-business owner with my husband. The idea of more free time to call my own seemed like an incredible gift.

As the kids began to move out of the house to pursue their educations, a home once filled with the noise and chaos of six people shrank down to a quieter household. Time freed up, and I realized I had an opportunity to begin to fill in my life. The problem? I was so busy looking after everyone else that I'd completely neglected myself and the things that brought me joy.

I became restless, as the reality of the changes came upon me.

Restless, unsettled, and unhappy.

It was the unhappiness that puzzled me. Didn't I have everything to look forward to? Wasn't this my time? There were no resounding reasons to be unhappy, yet I was, and uncertain about what to do with any of it.

As uncomfortable as those feelings were, I stayed with them to try and get to the why behind them. By not numbing out or trying to bury those feelings, I was taking the first steps towards owning my life and choosing self-leadership.

Now, it's your turn. Are you ready to dig in? Are you ready to explore what's working and what isn't? When we are younger, we often see opportunity and space for creation but as adults fall out of practice with embracing the unknown.

Restlessness is an invitation for change. For it to be meaningful and truly life-enhancing, however, requires returning to a state of introspection and questioning. We must invite curiosity and uncertainty. It may even mean straddling the arenas of intellectual, emotional, physical, and spiritual desires.

Restlessness pushes you to action and to accept, wholeheartedly, full responsibility for your life. It's the ultimate liberation to create your life, as only you can.

Part of the trip into creating the life you want is accepting that there will be times of discomfort. But there are also unexpected experiences filled with wonder and joy.

Even in our darkest times, it is possible to reach out and find just the right person, book, or thought that will help bring us one step closer to our unknown destination.

## Dismantling Myths about Change

Most of us would say we don't like it when change is afoot, fear it even. Is this in fact true, or is this a story? An easy, if unsatisfying, means of staying within our comfort zone—that we have concocted as adults?

Think about babies; they experience all kinds of change. The physical, of course as they are growing and learning in countless ways. But part of that is due to being restless.

Consider that there's no good reason for a baby to move from sitting to standing. Sitting, they are fully catered to. Needs are met, people come to the baby. But there's an internal push, a drive to become more independent and explore on their own. Once on their feet, they see more and put together some of the sounds they've heard. The internal pressure to move towards those sights and sounds makes them restless.

They begin to make efforts to walk. First, safely around the furniture, but then, there's a gap. They may choose to plop down on their bottoms and crawl that space, but soon crawling becomes too slow. Inevitably, they take the chance to cross the gap on their feet. Also, inevitably, they fall. And yet, up they get and try again; the drive of restlessness is strong. They are designed for growth and movement and so are we.

Babies do the hard work, the showing up and pushing forward, but it's important to note that there's a lot of support along the way. Parents, grandparents, and others are cheering them on with smiles, nods, outstretched arms, and positive words. When they take the inevitable tumble, the supporting cast is there to pick them up, give them a hug and then encourage them to try again.

To them, restlessness is a cue that it's time to start moving.

What causes adults to be restless? A change in our world, in our relationships, or even in ourselves. Sometimes it's boredom, when we know we have been doing too much of the same old thing.

Restlessness kicks in, inviting us to challenge ourselves. We get itchy to use more of our talents, to see what we are made of, and to expand our horizons. It's no different than when infants move from sitting to standing.

**"Healthy discontent is the prelude to progress."**

**Mahatma Gandhi**

Unlike babies, with their built-in support systems and willingness to see how far they can go, our adult selves may have limited amounts of both. So we plan and strategize. This isn't always a good thing.

While vision and planning are helpful, sometimes we go down the rabbit hole of overthinking. Trying to work out every possible scenario can effectively keep us on the sidelines. While waiting for everything to be in place and perfect, we do nothing.

When our restlessness is pulling us into unseen waters, part of the journey requires faith. We can only guess at the outcomes and must accept there will be unforeseen results. Embracing the unknown contributes to far happier and more energized feelings—the kind that will keep us moving forward.

# Chapter 2: Right Here, Right Now

**“Learn to get in touch with the silence within yourself and know that everything in this life has a purpose.”**

**Elisabeth Kubler-Ross**

When the first of the kids moved out of the house, there was a noticeable shift in the energy. One less person needing a ride, or voicing an opinion about chores, meals and opportunities to socialize with friends. Suddenly, there was a shift in interactions between the remaining members of the family. One person had moved on to explore more of her life outside the constraints of our family life. With her departure, everyone became more aware of their potential next steps.

Collectively, we began to consider exactly where we were in the here and now and what was and wasn’t working. To varying degrees, we all felt a desire to begin thinking beyond the everyday and into our futures.

To make the most of those restless feelings, we are best served to take some time to reflect on where we are, right here and right now. I think of this as X, as in X marks the spot on your personal life map.

Taking the time to stop and consider your location and position within your life will help formulate your vision.

Knowing my life was going to change significantly when our children all moved out, I realized it was time to take stock of the state of my life and determine what might be next.

This was a big challenge because there never was a plan for what would come next. Jobs, household tasks, parenting, older parents—somehow the time got away. We were working for someday but not "today," and we postponed having the conversations and goals that would get us to where we wanted to be. When the day finally came, we didn't know what to do.

It was time to exercise self-leadership. This is a skill I hadn't been taught growing up and one that is essential in crafting the life you want.

## Understanding Self-Leadership

Self-leadership is, essentially, learning how to take full responsibility for your life.

It's the willingness to stop any victim behaviours such as handing over decision making to others and then blaming them for the outcome. Or, it might be a perspective that bad things always happen to you and are out of your control. While for others it is about becoming a constant complainer and choosing to talk to everyone but the person with whom you have an issue. Victim behaviour is learned in childhood and while it may be comfortable because it is known, this way of living is one of the biggest means to hold yourself back. By choosing self-leadership, you accept that you have the ability to create change for yourself. It requires increasing your self-confidence and your self-awareness, both of which are possible once you decide to live a life aligned to your values.

The truth is that if you want things to be different, it is essential to take on a new behaviour. The exciting part is that you get to accept both the rewards and consequences of making your own decisions. While you might not quite know it yet, doing so feels amazing.

When I sat down and began looking at my life, I realized that I needed to be honest with myself. If I wasn't, I couldn't move forward. The echoing internal silence and my restlessness told me it was time.

So, what's the first step?

Take stock of your life, just as it is.

To do that, I have included some resources in the appendix. You'll need a notebook as you move through the questions. Your answers and what you discover will all help as you begin your journey.

To start, let's begin with an exercise you can use to assess your life satisfaction. In the appendix, you will find a chart called The Wheel of Life. This tool offers an easy view of where you are and where you wish to place your attention.

Next, it's time to define your values. These are the foundation to creating your vision and the goals that will take you there. We don't talk much about our values but knowing them is integral to understanding how and why you make your decisions.

Have you got your notebook? It's time to start filling the pages and creating your vision.

Can you name your top three values? If not, or if you need a reminder of what values are, see the appendix. By the way, as tempting as it is, you cannot ask other people what your values are. This is highly personal and only you can ultimately determine what motivates you to make decisions. Once you've listed your top three values, you're in a better position to decide what's next. Consider them your true north, as you begin to plot your course. Reviewing the Wheel of Life and your values list helps you see how closely the two match.

As you take stock of your life right now, just as it is, ask yourself this: what's the distance between what you've listed as your top values and your life satisfaction? I imagine you have a pretty good idea already, but getting your thoughts down on paper helps clear some of the mental frustration and serves as a reminder of your starting point.

## Accepting "What Is" Holds the Key for What Can Be

Once I began that journey of assessing where my life was and where I wanted it to be, I found that one of the statements I had to let go of was "it will be better when." Whatever you are completing this statement with, won't. That sentiment is a deferral that prevents us from taking control of what we want the outcome to be.

Prior to my marriage I had done a lot of travelling and looked forward to doing more of it as time and money were available. Unfortunately, this was an area that my husband and I never really discussed in any detail. I was happy to see more of Canada in our early years together but hadn't accepted that when my husband said he only wanted to travel in our own country, he was being totally honest. Somehow, I had deluded myself into believing that over time, he would be just as interested as I was in exploring other parts of the world.

Choosing to believe something else, telling myself that I could sell it to him in some way was not an honest representation of the situation. No matter how much I wanted it to be different, it was not going to be "better when," because he was telling me the truth.

Assessing "what is" right now gives you the clarity to begin to create your vision. Take some time with this. You might find it uncomfortable when you start removing the layers of excuses and victimhood and just stand quietly in the truth of your life.

Once again, it's notebook time.

Life truth questions: Do the people and the things in your life match your values?

What's working and what isn't?

If something isn't working, why isn't it? Do you know?

Asking "Do you know?" is a critically important question. Self-honesty takes courage. In this time of reflection and truth telling, look at everything. Leave no stone unturned: from leisure time to family time, planning for the future and making decisions about finances.

When I began the journey, I only knew some of the answers. The rest came later.

As you begin to ask these questions of yourself, be kind. Practice some self-compassion. This work is a little messy, especially as you start to see where you've lived up to your expectations and where you've let others determine the areas of how you live.

Whether you are single or in a relationship, assessing where you are and what you want lies squarely on your shoulders. Attempts to offload why you are or are not doing or living the life you want sets you back. If you don't own it, you can't have it. And yes, it might seem a bit overwhelming right now, but I promise, if you commit to this work, choose to take responsibility for your life, you truly will be able to craft your own journey of joy.

Speaking of joy, grab that notebook again and make a list of what you enjoy. Have some fun with this. It doesn't matter if you are doing it now or haven't done it for thirty years. Get it down on paper. And then make a list of what you might like to try. We'll get back to this later, but it's good to have a little fun on the journey, don't you think?

## X Marks the Spot(s)

Self-assessment, of where things are right now, is like marking an X on your own treasure map. This is your starting point but that X will move as you make decisions towards what you want your life to be. That's okay, it's called living.

You have made the decision to assess, you have answered some questions and you are ready to live a life more aligned with who you are and what you want. Great. Now what?

The first step is your willingness to recognize the truth of your current situation.

Take my desire to travel. My husband spoke his truth. The remaining choice was to accept what was and then decide what I would do. Not what I could convince or sell him on, but how I could make this desire happen for me.

When we are in relationships with others, one of the pitfalls can be trying to make everything a "we" when there are real advantages to creating individual experiences. This is how we continue to maintain our own identities and build lives of meaning in and out of our closest connections.

Accepting others for who they are is to offer respect and love. It's important you do the same for yourself. Wanting different adventures, different experiences, even if they didn't include him, was okay. Honoring myself and those dreams? Also 100% okay. Just because we are well-versed in thinking of everyone first, doesn't mean that needs to continue.

If being alone makes you shaky and uncertain, well, that's even more reason to cultivate activities that are solely your own. Building yourself up, becoming more solid in who you are, strengthens you and any relationships you are in. In my case, since travelling was important, the choice became not if, but how.

The second step is inviting your imagination to come and play. Sit by yourself. Open your notebook to a new page and describe in as much detail as you can, what your life would be like, if all the pieces were together in the way you wish. Consider your job, relationships—including your spouse/partner, kids, siblings, friends. How will you fill your spare time? What about your health? Do you have pets? What kind of home do you live in and where?

Write as quickly as you can, bypassing any negative thoughts. This is not the time to get lost in budgetary concerns. Nuggets of possibility exist within even the most "outlandish" thoughts. This is your chance to open yourself. Instead of denying or pushing away your hopes and dreams, allow them to emerge.

We do so much of this in our younger years. In part, due to our own uncertain future; but also because our lives stretch out in front of us. As time passes and we add in more people and responsibilities, our ideas of what could be go by the wayside. Happily, this enthusiasm comes back, if we make space for it.

Now that you have all that down, review your list. Consider where life doesn't match up to your hopes. No doubt there are gaps (you wouldn't be feeling restless if there weren't). Please don't get discouraged. Instead, think of this as the beginning of a grand adventure. One in which you are setting up your own points of interest and treasure chests. One in which you invite the whole you to come alive and fully participate. There will be some work to do before you have really gotten from this place to the one you are dreaming of. That's okay. It's part of the journey and one you will use again and again.

Just because you are choosing to own your life, doesn't mean you have to do it alone. In fact, we aren't meant to. Support is crucial, and it is part of the assessment you are going to do in figuring out where you are and where you want to be.

Big changes, where as much work happens inside as out, occur incrementally. There are people willing to help you, but you must ask.

The people who can best support you—your tribe—aren't always who you think they will be. That's okay too. Part of stepping up and owning your life is pushing yourself to engage with others.

Who then is an eligible tribe member? Who fits this role and might be someone you can lean on?

## Tribe Members Understand the Difference between Empathy and Sympathy

One marker of those able to see you through is that they understand the difference between empathy and sympathy.

Empathy connects because it demonstrates the ability to share your space and offer understanding of your efforts, even when they cause distress or emotional pain. It doesn't require them to have experienced your situation, but rather they are willing to stay with you while you travel the journey. Instead of offering solutions, they offer companionship so that you know you are not alone. To be offered understanding without judgement or expectations is an emotional gift beyond measure.

Sympathy on the other hand is a bit like getting a pat on the head. The person offering sympathy stands outside of your emotional pain and often chooses to speak platitudes. Even if it is meant kindly, it lacks the emotional connection in which you feel supported.

When you begin trying out self-leadership by taking on new behaviours and ways of doing things, you need to surround yourself with people to whom you can turn for assistance. This new path is work and like anything important it is best done in the company of those who wish to see you succeed. They are your tribe.

Seek out those who shared some of their story with you and have grown into their lives. Hopefully, someone in your family can be a member, although it is not necessary. Consider a friend or co-worker with whom you have connected. And don't discount a minister or member of the clergy, if you belong to a religious community. By way of their profession, they are often great resources.

## Tribe Members Allow You to Be as You Are

The key is to find a few people who allow you to feel what you feel and think what you think. Some will be in your community, but it is also possible to connect via technology. I have done this and cherished all those who, at various times in my life, have seen me through difficult times. It is also one of the reasons I offer mentoring because I have experienced more growth in a shorter period when I have sought a trusted advisor. Sometimes we need to bolster support outside of our regular community. Regardless of our age, we all need support. Every time there is a transition, either internal or external, having support is imperative. It is also important to become a part of someone else's circle. Be present in your transition and know that there are others who are also looking for support and understanding. One of the most uplifting things you can do for yourself is to find the courage and compassion to extend a helping hand to others.

And, if you need help, I'm only a call or email away.

## Learning to Live from the Passenger's Seat

When I completed the questions above, I had many hard truths to face and even more questions about how my life had become so much less than what I had hoped for decades before.

When you think about your life, where do you see yourself in relationship to others and to what you want from life? Do you see yourself as living as the passenger or the driver? Do you prefer to sit in silence as opportunities arise, or do you take a chance on stepping up?

Many of us, by circumstance or experience learn to become passengers and live by default. Over time, that becomes comfortable. We choose to be there, because we don't trust our abilities, or we are afraid of failing. Instead of trusting ourselves to make things happen, we wait for the sure thing.

Does that sound like you? Have you been firmly living the passenger life?

When we operate our lives by allowing others to make decisions for us, we may find ourselves further and further from where we once imagined we could be. And, in order to make peace with our drifting, we may even convince ourselves that we are perfectly happy as things are. Until we aren't. Until restlessness and disquiet take up more and more of our internal space.

Perhaps, like me, you are questioning why those other people have been able to "make it happen". Their life seems to flow in a straight line, while yours is filled with uncertainty and false starts. You ask yourself, what do they have that you don't? Are they smarter, more able, or more talented?

As I watched the forward movement of others, I wondered how they had such a certainty of purpose, when I had none. How, I wondered, had they done so?

I had been frustrated for much of my life, unable to nail down where my talents lay. I lacked the certainty to create a vision for myself and the kind of life I wanted to live.

When I finally had the courage to consider what I wanted for my life, the searching began, along with all those questions you answered above. There were two burning questions which I wrestled along the way: why and how. Why took me deep into an examined life and how helped me answer the questions to creating the satisfying and joy filled life I lead now. The one that is possible for you, if you go the distance.

As I further considered why it had taken me so long to find my way, I began to ask more questions of myself. Why hadn't I been able to determine a vision beyond wanting to be a parent and raise happy, functioning people? That was and remains a worthy goal, but it failed to bring me fully into the world. Where had my dreams gone and why?

## Outside Looking In

One of the first places we learn to live as passenger, rather than driver is from within the family, where we learn all our foundational development structures. As an introvert, my nature is to observe before acting. This is neither positive nor negative, unless it keeps me out of the mainstream of those around me.

I grew up in a large family, the fifth of six children and the second of three girls. Middle-middle you might say. On the outside looking in, our family seemed to have it all. We were fortunate in many ways, owing to the success of our family business. Yet, like many other families, what was viewed on the outside was not the reality on the inside.

I witnessed the emotional abuse of my mother by my father and then later my brothers. Despite her intelligence and many accomplishments in the community, my mother was crushed over time by the unrelenting dismissal of the intellectual and emotional respect she deserved.

For reasons I will never know, the discord between my parents carried over to me. As the target of bullying within my family, I came to see myself as deeply flawed. I was targeted by my brothers with a different form of emotional abuse than was aimed at my mother. Offhand critical and dismissive physical comparisons between myself and younger sister and the adoption of a “boy's” nickname resulted in an identity crisis of sorts—more gender resistant than gender confusion.

My love of the outdoors, the natural world, and reading—rather than more feminine activities like playing with dolls or wearing dresses—placed me even further from my dad's affection. I felt invisible to my father and an object of ridicule by my brothers. Accepting that I was a “less than” version of girlhood, I turned my back on many of the more feminine expressions expected. If I didn't participate, I wouldn't have to face the invisibility of my situation. I couldn't change it, so I learned how to give up. This is the antithesis of the perseverance needed in our everyday lives.

I also lacked the sense of belonging that we expect to have from within our families and which, from an evolutionary standpoint, is needed for survival.

Within my family, I grew up lonely, which was compounded by a family struggling with worsening alcoholism. Within our strict family code, the message was clear: What happens in the family, stays in the family. There were rings of isolation and ever-increasing dysfunction.

Finding myself more accepted outside my family than within it, I learned to travel on the fringes of groups and gatherings. Outside looking in. I interacted enough for some people to get to know me, but I let few get close. Now I understand that skating on the outside was part introverted nature and part protection.

What's a person to do when confronted with discontent and no reason to pin it to? Perhaps, like me, you begin to dig. To reflect and consider the options.

# Chapter 3: Growing Up Lonely

**"The wound is the place where the Light enters you"**

**Rumi**

"Does your family know you at all?"

This question was posed to Renee Cote by her husband after a visit with their young daughter. A visit in which she'd needed to establish some boundaries about her and her husband's parenting choices.

Unlike her parents, Renee and husband Patrick parent according to their values. Their parenting is based on distinct decisions around their shared parental leadership. Undoubtedly, Renee's parents found this odd, as their interactions within the family were mired in chaos.

Like so many others, Renee grew up in a home impacted by a parent struggling with depression, domestic violence, and emotional abuse. Her parents married young and didn't have the skills or knowledge about how to parent or communicate effectively.

As a child, Renee spent a lot of time alone, avoiding social interactions. Later, as she got older, she sought out others who talked and acted like she did. She understood them and they her. Most were also experiencing family violence. They understood each other, felt connected and in some ways, she'd found her own little family. One which mirrored some of the emotional abuse at home.

Unsurprisingly, Renee began drinking and doing drugs at an early age and often stayed out late at night. Those behaviours became her coping mechanisms, allowing her to stay out of the turmoil at home.

Over time, Renee grew what she terms "armor" as a self-protective measure.

"I had lots of self-hate and anger. I acted like things didn't bother me, that I didn't care."

That remained the case until Renee left home and sought help from a local women's shelter. It was then that she began to receive different messages and ideas of what her life could be like.

While Renee had created a persona of a tough outer armor, avoiding her home, I chose differently. I decided subconsciously that within the family, the safest course of action was to fly under the radar.

And in a very conscious bid for control, absolutely refused to drink or do drugs.

This made me a "dream teenager" but decidedly on the outside of many normal teen activities. To my peers I was the sunny happy person who got along with everyone. However, the alcoholism within the family, and the bullying my mother and I experienced were a quiet secret.

None of my peers knew the loneliness I felt.

## When You Grow Up Feeling on the Outside

Treated as a dreamy write-off by my family, my creative tendencies were dismissed. Rather than receiving messages of encouragement and support for my creative skills, I was instead reminded of the many ways I failed to measure up. As a child, then as a teenager and as a person. At a time when self-leadership is taught, when we are encouraged to create a vision, identify our values and set goals, I was left to my own devices. The lack of conversations about future directions coupled with underlying ridicule left me feeling confused and uncertain.

If we grow up being bullied, especially experiencing chronic bullying, the failure to change the outcome destroys our internal sense of control. Until we begin even small steps to effect change in our lives, we may continue to be victims of that story. The good news is that the small steps matter and so do our accomplishments in other areas of our lives.

## Bullied Child and the Adult Mental Health Consequences

Since my bullying was within my family, I created a double life.

In some areas, I was very successful. I gained a certain amount of popularity within my school community due to my involvement in sports, clubs, and school life in general. But I was noticeably lacking in self-confidence as a young woman. Too nervous and scared to be noticed and lacking any idea how to interact with the boys, I defaulted to friend. Tall, skinny, and wearing glasses, I believed I was unattractive and there was nothing I could do to change that.

Since I tried none of the usual methods of enhancing my attractiveness, nor did I ask for help to enhance my appearance, I created the truth that had been handed to me. My sister, in turn, lived out her truth. I watched as she dated my peers and eventually established a relationship with one of her classmates. Her success and my lack of success in this area further fueled my beliefs that I was flawed and unworthy.

One of the areas that I had to address as I sought to live a happier and more fulfilled life, was to give myself permission to ask for help. Prior to learning that this was okay, my belief system that I was on my own held me back over the years, in countless ways. From learning new skills, to trying new hobbies to advancing in a career, not asking for help kept me from truly reaching my potential.

Research published in the Lancet Journal of Psychiatry in 2015 tells us that fully one-third of children are bullied. Those who experience chronic bullying—more than six months—suffer the mental health consequences into adulthood. It is a form of trauma which affects brain function and development. Despite the chant to the contrary, it's not just sticks and stones which hurt you. As more studies are coming to the forefront, researchers better understand the impact of childhood bullying. Because we all believe that names don't "hurt", many of us are unaware of the lifetime impact.

Those of us who were bullied don't know we are part of such a large group, because one of the outcomes is feeling isolated. The research around the mental health outcomes such as anxiety, panic disorder, depression, and even thoughts of suicide explain the cascade of other adult outcomes. Everything from relationship, employment, and financial are all are poorer in comparison to those not bullied.

We live with feelings of shame which grow into beliefs of being flawed and unworthy of love and belonging.

Within my family, I felt all of that deeply. As such, my survival and coping mechanisms to try to control the outer chaos meant I was an avid rule follower, learned not to ask questions and worked hard at being a "good person." This made me something of a dream teenager from a parenting view. I didn't engage in much of the risky behaviour many teens fall into, but it added to my isolation within my peer group.

My non-teenage habits added to my overall feelings of isolation, even though by the end of my high school years I was invited to parties.

Living in an alcoholic household, I was familiar with what fall-down drunk looked like. I wanted none of that and so chose to be sober and continue the role of observer. It suited me, it was safe, and my friends accepted that they couldn't sway me.

Because I felt isolated, one of the obstacles I had to overcome was the sense of periphery belonging, the idea that I was on the edge of any group, rather than a part of it. This idea followed me through much of my life. It wasn't that the opportunity didn't exist, it was that I chose self-protection. Humour became one of my defense mechanisms, funny enough to engage, but also often self-deprecating. This helped me deflect attention and protect myself from having to chance rejection. For a long while, it was the only form of control over circumstances that I knew.

Cognitive and Social Neuroscientist John Cacioppo studies the role of connection and social isolation. As social animals, we are wired for connection. According to his work, isolation and feeling lonely don't just feel bad, they make us sick.

Feeling an outsider is problematic. Finding your tribe and expanding your social circle is not just a cultural need, it is a health need.

I can't help but think of my mom and her experiences of living in a small town. She was, in many ways, an activist, and her friendships reflected that. From creating programs for the elderly for their physical and mental health to bringing in adult education programs, she helped make things happen. Her primary friendships were with two women of similar education and interests. When one of her friends passed away and the following year the other moved out of the province with her husband, she was adrift. Her anchors were gone.

Perhaps she could have made new friends, but in a small rural farming community, there were not many opportunities to make connections. Since my father shared none of her goals or interests, and a very dysfunctional relationship had arisen between them, her spiral into loneliness and depression was heartbreaking. Succumbing to alcoholism, her life became smaller and smaller. Had she been able to create new friendships and resolve her marital problems, her outcome would have been different.

Research backs that up. In a TED talk, psychiatrist Robert Waldinger outlines the findings of a seventy-five-year study, which contained three key findings: "People who are more isolated than they want to be from others find that they are less happy, their health declines earlier in midlife, their brain functioning declines sooner, and they live shorter lives than people who are not lonely." Well that described my mom to a T. And, until I began to take stock of my life and make hard decisions, I was on track for those outcomes too.

When you know better, you can do better. That's important when crafting a life of meaning.

My mom's unhappiness contributed to giving me the courage, in my later years, to reject that outcome. Consciously or not, I had decided that I would not allow my life to follow hers. We were close, but my survival instinct and deep desire to live life fully kept me from following her path.

**"When you talk, you are only repeating what you already know. But if you listen, you may learn something new."**

**Dalai Lama**

As a child, I was the receptacle of other children's pain and confusion. My quietness invited them to share with me their lives and fears. From domestic violence to mental illness, all was shared. I didn't have any context in which to place such information, nor any resources to give; however, my listening was enough. In its own way, the pain-sharing was my connection to those around me. Perhaps this is why, even as a teenager, I could interact with diverse sets of groups. I accepted everyone for who they were, knowing that we have far more in common than we think.

Whether by design or default, the ability to be quiet and listen has become an important and valued skill. From strangers to life-long friends, people tell me their painful, confusing, and uncertain stories. Their intuition lets them know that I am "safe" and unlikely to judge. And I don't. I know how much I have struggled in this life and see that others do too.

We are all doing the best we can with what we know at any given time in our lives.

Part of my credo is that there is something to learn from everyone. The chance to give a measure of comfort by providing a listening ear and advice where requested underlines this belief. It is what brought me to including the role of Transition Mentor under my offerings. It's something I have done most of my life. Through my own journey to joy, I now know that I have more in my toolbox to offer than I did as a ten-year-old child.

More than ever, I see that the ability to listen is one of the greatest gifts any of us can provide. While some wish to call me wise, I think it only because I have, over the course of my life, listened to people struggling to make sense of their situations. I have learned from them and I have done my own work to heal from the emotional injuries I sustained while growing up.

Wisdom is knowledge applied. It is immensely satisfying to help others find their wisdom and act according to their needs. What I was missing myself, I give to others.

The other side of the quiet coin, however, was protection. This is part of an old habit of flying under the radar. As a child, this had become a reliable way to prevent unwanted shaming and hurtful comments. I found ways to be seen, but I limited opportunities of interaction to that of confidante.

As high school ended, and others were making choices about careers, I drifted. I would joke with a few of my friends that I couldn't seem to figure out what I wanted to be when I grew up. There were no signs that I could see pointing me in any one direction. I longed for purpose and direction but had none.

Feeling on the outside is a lonely place to be. I continued to feel that where and how I most wanted to be connected, I was not. The search continued, as I became more aware that it wasn't just purpose and direction I was seeking, but a sense of place. Of belonging.

While it is normal to feel alone during adolescence, those feelings were amplified for me. Our first place of belonging is within our families, and much like Renee, I did not belong in mine.

## Searching for Belonging

As I ventured out into the world, I was drawn to those who seemed to be connected in loving and healthy ways. I wanted that too, but I did not know how to obtain it. I didn't realize that my guidance system and perceptions of healthy loving relationships were based on bad information.

I translated different as better, and when I attended a friend's wedding and met the groom's family, they seemed to embody all the things I longed for. I wanted to be a part of that family dynamic. I hit it off with their eldest son, who shared my interests in the natural world and outdoor activities. Looking back, I realize that in some ways I fell in love with my perception of his family, as much as with him.

Their get-togethers gave me a new model to consider, and it seemed like a good one. The siblings all liked each other, and they were respectful and loving towards their mom. Their family activities didn't have an alcohol component, which seemed odd to me at the beginning, since every one of mine did.

There were differences, of course, and things about my own family of origin that I enjoyed and were missing in this one. However, I felt accepted and liked. The lure of belonging was immense.

Finding another person also eager to move our lives ahead, to fulfill our cultural vision of marriage and family, we married a year after meeting. Act in haste, regret in leisure. This old wisdom would have served me well, if I had been willing to listen.

The honeymoon phase exists in relationships of all kinds, intimate and work. It's that time when all is fresh and new and none of the day-to-day activities have lost their rosy glow. The time comes, however, when everyday demands create a little strain or present a twist. Maybe we are required to voice an opinion or make a request we haven't yet had to make.

I had, for all intents, married my in-laws as well as my husband. So, when I started to exert some personal preferences, the true nature of the family culture arose. Every group has rules and expectations about behavior. I came to realize that what I saw as connection was just another version of managing dysfunction. In my family, it had been every man for himself and find the weakest link. In this one, a united team in which there were very clear rules to belonging, there was little-to-no room for changes. It looked different, but the demands were the same: Conform, or we will shame you into it.

My shame mindset was extremely well developed, and so I accepted the subtle and overt hints that the way I was needed to be improved. Information I had shared about my pain of growing up was used as a means of judgment. In their view, the way I thought and my desires of how to live were incorrect. The comments hurt, but I really wanted to be loved and longed to belong.

I tried hard to become something other than who I was. As you can imagine, the more I submerged the elements of who I was, the more stress and unhappiness it caused for both me and my husband. I could not maintain the efforts to change and become more "acceptable" in his eyes or those of his family. His efforts to "help" me just left me feeling worse about myself.

For the tribe I wanted so badly to belong to, it appeared as if I wasn't trying or didn't care about them. I wanted to be accepted for who I was, and they wanted me to be the type of person that fit into their mold. The harder I tried to be acceptable, the further I got from myself and from doing the things I enjoyed, the further I got from holding and creating the place from which self-leadership and vision are created.

It was truly a no-win situation. It caused years of emotional pain.

## Neglect "Me Time" and Risk Losing Your "Want To"

If self-leadership pivots on the ability to formulate a vision for your life, how do you overcome the idea that what you have to offer is neither special nor important? I believe you start by creating "me time," doing what you enjoy.

How does creating a vision or a goal help someone who is trying to build his or her life?

Me time is not selfish time, nor is it a wasted effort. It is time that I've come to discover is quite important to bringing the best of yourself forward into the world and into the lives of the people you care about. I didn't always know this.

Upon the arrival of my first born and lacking the support or proximity of extended family, parenting was a twenty-four-hour, seven-day-a-week job. My husband had a demanding job, limited hours, and an even more limited idea of his place as a parent.

New to the area, I lacked women friends and family. It was, as you can imagine, an incredibly challenging time. Not just because of the role shifts, but because the thing I needed most, me time, was a gaping hole.

In her book The Happiness Project, Gretchen Rubin talks about the importance of women friends. She emphasizes that time spent with them is important to both a woman and the man with whom they are in a relationship. Apparently, we are less lonely and happier when we spend time with other women.

While I certainly loved my children, the 24/7 parenting took its toll. The adage, all work and no play makes a dull girl or boy, is true of us all.

When we take on all our roles—parent, wife, community member, employee—and forget about the one constant within them, the me, we neglect the very part of ourselves that has to show up and expend energy.

Engaging in me time means putting aside all the should do, ought to, and must do and inserting, from time to time, want to.

Want to is an underutilized phrase because it feels, well, selfish. Doesn't it? I want to take a bath, lock the door, light candles, and read a book. I want to call a friend, go to a craft show/concert/gallery/coffee shop or whatever and be...me. When we do that, we keep the relationship with ourselves going.

We keep alive the spark and flame that fans the traits that are uniquely us. If and when we don't, we can arrive at the other side of a relationship—marital, parental, or personal—and not have any idea of how to answer the want to option.

If you neglect "me time" then you risk losing the answer to "want to". And when you lose that answer it becomes very difficult to create the vision of what's next for your life.

# Chapter 4: Flawed

**"Make your own recovery the first priority in your life."**

**Robin Norwood**

Tell me, how often does a nagging internal voice come to visit you? You know the one I mean- the inner critic. It's the one that urges you to put aside your dreams and live the easy life. It usually arises when you are pursuing something you care about and putting yourself out into the world more fully. It is a keen ally to a bully because it backs up their message of inferiority.

Learning to see and overcome the inner critic is one of the first hurdles to achieving anything of merit.

Distractions, doubts, and, yes, even despair, can have us second-guessing whether the path we have chosen is worth continuing.

The inner critic is very crafty at whispering unkind and cruel comments.

It's also good at discounting personal success and how our work benefits others. Finding the means to meet and beat the inner critic is an ongoing battle.

Be it athlete, scholar, craftsman, or artist, our work can only improve by the day-in and day-out doing of it. As we do, we continue finding new challenges to meet and ways to grow, change, and learn.

All the things the inner critic fights hardest against.

Falling victim to constant comparing is a second hurdle and further outcome of living with criticism. You learn to see the world and those around you as a measure of what you have and what they have. Social media feeds often have us questioning the success of our relationships, financial status, and overall life satisfaction.

It's an easy step onto the scarcity plain in which we fail to appreciate the abundance of our lives; leading us down the slippery slope of judging ourselves and others.

The unconscious growth of comparison and judgmental attitudes can creep up on us, and it will continue to our detriment, if we don't catch ourselves.

## "Should-ing" on Others

Spending time in nature is one of my favourite means of grounding myself and letting go of everyday stresses. I immerse myself in the sights, smells, and sounds around me. I have a set of trails that I especially enjoy and, depending on the time of day and year, see almost no one else. I engage all my senses and am technology-free while I do so. In my heart, this experience is the right way to be there.

That sentiment—"the right way" thinking—is ripe for judgment, as I found on one warm spring day.

Venturing out on a weekend to my favorite hiking spot, I found many others also out to enjoy nature time. The trails were busy with people of all ages out experiencing a break from the city. Many were engaged in conversations with their children or as couples. Some walked quietly and pointed out things of interest as they came upon them. Others stopped to take pictures or to read the information about the flora and fauna.

At one point on the trail, I saw a woman who seemed completely out of place. She was walking briskly, made no eye contact, had "gym" wear on, and sported ear buds from which I could hear thumping music. My first thought was, "You are completely missing the point of being out here, why even bother?" I felt both pity and disdain that she was so disconnected from her surroundings.

Then I realized how judgmental that was. I had created my own "how to" of hiking, but that was by no means the only way. I was imposing my "should" and musts upon her, with no idea of what it was she was using this time for or what she needed from it. My experience, I realized, doesn't have to be her experience.

I am grateful I crossed paths with her. Even though we didn't speak, she provided a very powerful reminder of how we can pollute not just our lives, but those of others, with our rigid views of the world.

## Mindset. How We Think Matters, Part One

Judgment tends to put us on unconscious guard, vigilant for spotting all the things that are wrong in the world.

Passing judgment or being judgmental becomes an everyday companion, doling out right/wrong, good/bad, deserving/undeserving and any number of other scenarios. It comes from a fixed mindset, a belief system guiding us on everything from activities of merit to validation of our pursuits and abilities.

Mindsets are, as you may gather, the way that we think about the world, others, and ourselves.

Dr. Carol Dweck's research explains the difference between a fixed mindset and a growth mindset. In a nutshell, those with a fixed mindset believe they are born with fixed abilities and talents. Essentially, you have it or you don't and effort will not make an appreciable difference. People with a fixed mindset are more likely to settle and less likely to challenge themselves, because they fear failure. They see failure as personal, rather than as something that doesn't work out and is worth trying again.

I think it's safe to say that the shame mindset is a subset of the fixed mindset. It's debilitating and keeps us very small, afraid to venture out into the world. We most definitely do not want to be put back into the firing range of ridicule or embarrassment. My coping strategy of flying under the radar, while safe, was also very limiting.

Part of what kept me small and seeking safety also had to do with the negative soundtrack that ran through my mind. You might be familiar with it. It's where the "not enoughs" live.

One of the most challenging aspects of creating a bigger life is confronting all the "nots" that lie buried within us. Often, we are unaware of how many there are, how deeply buried, and how much we let them impact our lives. Not good enough, not smart enough, not strong enough, not pretty/handsome enough, not talented enough—not, not, not. Compress the phrase and it is "not enough."

When you grow up in a world of judgment, criticism, comparison, and indifference, you construct stories of your importance in the world. Who you are and what you are capable of. You create a fixed mindset, worry about failure, and choose to manage your life by staying in the comfort zone.

Without positive input from others, these ideas continue to create self-limiting beliefs. These, in turn, narrow your life vision. A narrowed vision puts you at risk of trying to prove your importance in the world and to yourself.

What do we do to try to prove that we are enough? In North America, we keep busy.

For some, being busy is a badge of honor. It's used as a means of self-validation, self-worth, and side-stepping reflective moments. It has become a culturally embedded form of value. I think it also contributes to a disconnect from life.

Working for the greater good and being a contributing member of one's community are worthy ways of spending your time. They can, sometimes, also be handy screens, preventing you from really seeing what's going on behind it all.

In the story The Wizard of Oz, the great and powerful Oz seemed to control everything, but really controlled nothing at all. He created an illusion of having it together through bells, whistles, and bright lights. There was action and movement, but in no direction.

Busyness, especially if it is for the sake of others, might equal value—to yourself or to your perceived position within a group. Busyness can also be a means of numbing out whatever else is going on. Being on all the time, being available or doing anything at all, means there is no time for reflection. Reflection is the quiet space where you check in with yourself and take the pulse of how you are doing and how things are with your relationships and with yourself.

The busy badge of honour keeps you from being fully who you are. It is also a marker about how you find your self-worth and how you judge the worth of others. Being busy can be as much of an addiction as eating, texting, social media, smoking, or drinking. It is an attempt to deflect thoughts that may feel too uncomfortable to explore. It just happens to be culturally accepted.

## Status Quo Is an Abyss

You know the place I mean. It's when we quit thinking about what if and sink into good enough. It's watching reruns of television shows, getting lost in the antics of media-made celebrities who model the behaviour of self-centered children, adding nothing to life.

Status quo is choosing inertia instead of activities requiring you to show up and be seen. The abyss invites you to stay put and ignore opportunities to enrich your life and the lives of others.

Instead of being interested, curious, and ready to create some new thing, connection, or thought, we are content to stay in the box of the known.

Have you noticed the people who exist within that box? Their eyes are dead, their features flat, and their energy is a dark hole sucking the life out of those around them.

They're everywhere.

They are the parents tied to a cell phone, pushing a stroller and ignoring the little spark of life in front of them.

They are couples at dinner unable to hold a conversation, so they escape to technology or stare silently at their food.

## A Life without Vision Is a Life Destined to Drift

How does this happen? Where does the possibility of a life to be explored and experienced disappear to? It disappears through a death by a thousand things purchased and few providing lasting enjoyment.

Or maybe it is the illusion of connection without being in the moment with the person or people right here, with you.

Have you deluded yourself into thinking that you know everything you are capable of learning? Have you accepted that new is only as portrayed by the stuff you buy rather than the knowledge you accumulate or the limits to which you push yourself emotionally and physically?

These are the attitudes and behaviours of people with a fixed mindset. Inertia is self-perpetuating.

Being in transition is about being in a state of decision-making. It's the process of trying to make sense of a series of choices that appear to make no sense at all but that we know are going to result in change. When we say yes to change, make decisions that affect the trajectory of our lives, we are accepting the unknown.

Say no to fear and yes to possibility. Fear tells us, "No good will come of that, stay here." Possibility says, "I don't know what the outcome will be, but I believe good things are possible."

We don't always realize when we are listening to one or the other. We can get a lot of advice from friends, family, and even our own life experiences and goals.

We frequently try to make important decisions by creating a list of pros and cons, outcomes and consequences, or some other form of flowsheet thinking. Data in, data out. We want to avoid being wrong, but what's wrong for one person isn't necessarily wrong for another. Much of what we get from family, friends, and even the community at large is based on their own abilities to grapple with fear and possibility.

If you talk to two people who almost drowned, you may hear two different opinions about learning to swim. One of them might say, "Don't go in the water; it's dangerous." The other might say, "After that experience, I wanted to learn how to swim, and I found I really loved it."

I have listened to both opinions. Fear nearly crushed my artistic potential; possibility has expanded my world in ways my vision didn't even include.

Listening to other people is a way to gather information, even perspective, but it should not be the deciding factor.

How do you get from A to B, fear to possibility? Get quiet, get by yourself, and get honest. Gut feelings, the whispers of intuition, are your magnetic north. If you are feeling pulled in a direction, if the idea repeatedly occurs, that's what you need to pay attention to. In Chapter 1 I asked you to make a list of things you enjoy, or recall enjoying. Pull it out and have a look, add to it if you like. What do you see there? What is calling for attention?

It might be to pick up the paint brush, begin the music project, have the hard conversation, apply to school, don't go to school, settle down, or cut all your ties. No one can know what dream or opportunities are waiting for you to choose. Only you.

Everyone has opinions, only you know your truth. The question really becomes then: Are your ears open to fear or to possibility?

Change is uncomfortable because it is unknown but staying where you are can be even more painful.

Dr. Brené Brown's research on shame and vulnerability shows that as women, an ongoing myth around the illusion of effortless multi-tasking takes a toll. It separates us from others, and it keeps us from making real connections.

Asking for help shouldn't be shame-inducing, especially as we consider that making changes to our lives usually requires help.

When you become serious about changing your life, becoming the creator of your own experience, then you must pause, step back, and be willing to draw back the screen of your own Oz and see what's there.

We all have stories, and those stories define us. We give them meaning and tell ourselves what kind of people we are through them. If we never visit them, never give them light, they can turn into a dark and somewhat nasty character. Kind of like Gollum in The Lord of the Rings stories.

A fixed mindset creates specific and limiting rules. It tells us who we are and what we will or won't try. It's all based on the idea of being a natural or not.

It also has carries messages about failure and success.

Among the many things I wish I had learned younger and better is how to use failure as a teacher, instead of considering it a personal weakness. Let's face it, from the moment we enter school, and sometimes before, the last thing we want to do is "fail."

Regardless of the area—from relationships to business ventures—failure, even the idea of it, is cringe worthy. It can keep us from trying and it can keep us from stopping, even when we know we should.

"Fear, embarrassment, and intolerance of failure drives our learning underground and hinders innovation.

No more. Failure is strength. The most effective and innovative organizations (people) are those that are willing to speak openly about their failures because the only truly 'bad' failure is one that's repeated." (Admitting Failure.org)

## Before the Pinnacles of Success Were the Thousand Tries

Our cultural mindset is one of stark contrasts—win/lose, success/failure, strong/weak, healthy/sick. There are no gray areas: You are one or the other, and there are clear messages about what side to be on. We have many stories of success, but what we get is the result. What is missing is what happened before the big contract, the gold cup, or the breakthrough innovation. We see and hear about the pinnacles and not the thousand tries that required starting again. Perhaps just as importantly, we are missing what was learned from those failures.

What kind of failures have pushed along my personal growth? Academic, for one.

As an adult I returned to university with a plan to change careers and become an ESL (English as a Second Language) teacher. I had completed all my course work and the last component was in the classroom with a supervising teacher. I was nervous, as many new teachers are, and I was intimidated. In part because I found the teacher to have an abrupt and even condescending manner with her students. Not at all what I was expecting.

When it came time for me to begin teaching under her tutelage, I struggled with finding the means to discuss my progress with her. My natural tendency to sit back and let someone else take the lead was heading into an increasingly difficult and negative direction.

I began to realize that she was not fulfilling her end of the partnership. As my teaching progressed, we had yet to meet to discuss either my lesson plan or her feedback as to my performance. Just as any situation in which you choose to put off a much -needed conversation, my teaching and our interpersonal relationship suffered.

I had unconsciously reverted to my childhood self, feeling intimidated and powerless. Instead of asking for those meetings, I chose to hunker down and just try to get through the placement. Trying to skirt the issue built a bad situation into a worse one. Imagine my horror when I realized the very real possibility that she was going to fail me, without ever having a conversation with me about her concerns.

Indeed, that was exactly what happened. I received a letter from the university letting me know that the supervising teacher had given her evaluation that I was not a competent teacher and gave me a failing grade. I was mortified, especially when my supervising professor shared that the teacher had also felt compelled to write a separate letter to the dean of the department. In that letter she suggested that if I was the quality of student they were putting through their program, that the program was flawed and should be revised.

I felt sick to my stomach. Mortified, embarrassed and very, very angry.

She failed me both literally and figuratively, and I failed myself by not overcoming my discomfort to have the conversation I intuitively knew needed to happen and didn't. From that experience, that failure, I have learned how to have crucial conversations. It was a difficult but life-changing lesson. My life has improved because of it.

(And yes, I did my placement again, with a different teacher who understood her role and from whom I learned much. I passed the course, becoming a certified teacher of ESL).

**"Many of life's failures are people who did not realize how close they were to success when they gave up."**

**Thomas Edison**

The more important something is, the more we attach it to our self-worth and resist admitting failure, and, more importantly, the greater we resist re-framing it as a chance to learn something new about ourselves, the organization, or someone else.

What is failure anyway? Is it an attempt or effort that didn't have the desired outcome? That's it, isn't it? It seems to me that if we don't admit our failures, then any efforts are half of what they could be. Big innovations need the willingness to "be all in," as a friend of mine is fond of saying. Give it your all and be willing to stand by the outcome, whatever or wherever that takes you.

## What's Important about Failure?

So, what about failure is important? Ownership and responsibility for starters. Each allows us to create new chances for great things. The embarrassment factor is pretty huge on failure. The more our ego is invested, the bigger the mountain to climb when we pick ourselves up and face what went wrong. I believe that we sometimes experience versions of the same kind of failure until we really learn the lesson we need to. My failures have taught me the importance of speaking up for myself, to voice a concern, or to ask for clarity.

## With the Right Attitude, Failure Expands Our Life

In my personal life, the ending of my marriage could be considered a failure. Speaking to other people who have divorced I discovered other people who have changed their minds on that. Now, I see it as a tremendous chance for personal growth. Even though it was difficult, it encouraged me to expand into the life I wanted and was not going to achieve within that relationship.

Learning has been fueled by the experience of ending and, even more importantly, starting over. I learned more about grief and loss. I came to value patience. I came to also value acceptance for where I have control (me) and where I don't (others). Healing old wounds, honoring skills and talents, trying new interests, and expanding my world are all outcomes of what in the past would be considered a failure.

Without mistakes, errors, and failures, there would be no new ideas or things for us to discover. This is true personally and within organizations.

Just like judgment, the shame around failure requires energy to maintain. That's where self-talk comes into play.

## Introducing Negative Nelly

Ideally, as a child or young adult, we'd have an adult who helps us understand and internalize obstacles and successes to overcoming them. Positive self-talk messages transform into a positive self-image and the belief of self-reliance and capability.

If we don't, if a nasty Negative Nelly continues to pick at us any time we dare to stretch our wings, there is another way to put her meanness to bed. How?

We start with noticing our negative self-talk.

Start with mistakes. We all make them. "Listen" to the words of your internal dialogue. Do words like stupid, idiot, or moron come up, and are they preceded with I am?

Or what about an idea to create or do something new? Do the not enoughs come into your thoughts? That would be such fun, but I am not…young enough, smart enough, good enough, etc.

Take a step back. Would you say these things to your child, your friend, or your partner? With a fixed mindset, you might. But with a growth mindset, likely not. We could not imagine being that cruel or unkind. But as for ourselves, we are fair game.

All these nots, negativity, and decidedly unloving patterns of self-talk keep us from creating a bigger life.

What I find especially interesting is the pervasiveness of the inner critic and negative self-talk. This is so even among people you would never expect.

"Down a dark desert highway..."

Yes, the beginnings of a hit song, by a group I enjoy. When news came of the death of the band's founding member, Glenn Frey, I was reminded of a documentary I saw about his band. There was a moment in it when I realized that I had something in common with them, and you might too.

Despite their plentiful hits, when they were getting back together and beginning to write, they were afraid. Did they still have it? Could they still work together? Would the outcome be up to the previous work?

If you've ever tackled anything that is going to be out there for the world to see, you probably know what I'm talking about. When I am writing for work, the doubts don't arise. I just get the job done. The fear demon doesn't raise its red-eyed, toothy, bad-breathed self. It's just me and my computer, and it's off to the races.

But, if it's me and my prose, whoa, that's a whole other story. Somehow, it's comforting to know that there are accomplished musicians and writers—anyone taking the journey of expression—who face the "not good enough monster" and do it anyway.

I think Yoda (sparked by another creative type) would famously say, "Do or do not. There is no try."

## Choosing to Persist

A necessary part of the equation within self-leadership is learning the importance of perseverance, of grit. Angela Duckworth wrote an entire book on the subject. Within the realm of creating lives, transforming them even, nothing can match the decision to stick with it. Perseverance is a hallmark characteristic of the growth mindset. Perseverance is the willingness not just to try again, but to find the lesson in the failure. Examining what didn't work and then adjusting your next effort.

Is there anything more worthwhile than overcoming our fears of not good enough and choosing instead to see where our talents and interests might take us?

I grew up with the expectations from some of the adults in my family that I'd never really accomplish much. As a result, instead of learning grit or how to persevere, I learned how to give up. I was surrounded by people rooted in a fixed mindset, who lived by the ideas of natural talent or inherent intelligence. Rather than encouraging me to try, they accepted when I gave up.

The great news is that as adults, we can, whatever our age, decide to overthrow those limiting beliefs.

Just because we may have given up on ourselves in the past, doesn't mean we need to now. If restlessness has come knocking at your door, see it as an invitation to create a life of real meaning and deep satisfaction. Perhaps in ways you never expected.

Not only can we learn, we are able to make things happen for ourselves. We can reach out and get the help we need rather than being stuck as the children we were, waiting for others to act in our best interests.

In a very real sense, asking for help when you have been conditioned to see it as weak is an act of bravery.

# Chapter 5: Striving to Be Enough

**"In a dark time, the eye begins to see."**

**Theodore Roethke**

When you grow up feeling as if you have limited value, you begin chasing worthiness. This can be found in how you spend your time, how much you do for others, the projects you take on, and the behaviours you display and are willing to accept.

Many of us—especially women and not just Canadians! — believe being nice and endlessly giving of ourselves is how we show that we're good, caring people. But giving more is not necessarily good. It certainly isn't if you must scramble to arrange other parts of your life, often impacting others' lives as well.

As a former over-giver, I was entrenched in the give 'til it hurts model. Usually, resulting in my being the one who was hurt.

Saying yes to others often meant I was saying no to me and, in the ripple effect, my family. I'd apologize to others, if I put them out, had to ask them to re-arrange their schedules, or if I had to say no. I didn't know that the lack of boundaries affected every area of my life. I had to learn about what was and wasn't negotiable.

## How Strong Boundaries Create Self-Worth

The move from people pleaser to standing firm within yourself offers substantial growth towards self-value and self-worth. It isn't easy to accomplish this when so much of our messaging tells us differently.

Our cultures, society, and religious beliefs tell us how we must show love and caring and how to be "good." We have many, many messages about how to give, but not very many about how to receive. The journey to learning a different way to live and even to think is found in many places. Mine came about during a year of cascading losses.

The year 2001 is etched in many people's minds due to the attacks in the US and while I too remember that time, it was my own personal voyage into darkness that became a pivotal life shift.

That year was the worst and most transformative year of my life. In the space of six months, I lost three women members of my family: my mother, a cherished aunt, and a sister. Those deaths and the changes resulting from them challenged some of my core beliefs.

When it comes to life lessons and changing old ideas, you are sometimes forced to face down what you believe about yourself and what you value. Sometimes they come in small interactions with others. Sometimes they come from dark nights of the soul.

My sister and I had moved far from our family of origin, and we'd never shared a close relationship. She'd been a party to the in-family bullying, but family is family and we spent some traditional holidays together. It was enough so that when she received her diagnosis of Stage IV cancer, I immediately thought how I could best support her.

She was a single mom, and her ex-husband was often not available due to mental health and addiction issues. She had close friends, some of whom went above and beyond traditional support, but it was still evident to me that her children were not getting the attention they needed.

Despite my strained feelings towards my father and sister, I felt my duty was to support them and her children the best I could. Over that six-month period, I chose to become the primary emotional support of her children, our newly widowed father, and her.

Even though my husband and I had our own seasonal business, which was at the height of the sales cycle, I chose to put the needs of my sister and her children first. For weeks at a time, I lived away from my own family, so I could care for her and her children. I also served as the information broker to the rest of our family, advising them of changes and updates to her health.

At the time, I felt there was little choice. Living out the good girl/good daughter upbringing was all too familiar to me. My own children were left to deal with this emotional situation largely on their own, as their father was working non-stop. His emotional intelligence was poor, and his ability to act on the needs of our children was strained. The fact that I wasn't there to bridge the deficit weighed heavily on me.

Better boundaries and greater self-worth would have helped me consider alternatives to giving up so much of mine and my family's mental welfare. It was done with the best of intentions, but the consequences of spending the better part of six months away from my own children and husband were great. It didn't serve any of us well.

I was giving all I had to give, with a limited support system. I lacked relief from the emotional strain and was still reeling from the losses of mother and aunt. To say my mental state was taxed is a fair assessment.

One of the fallouts of this decision was me being inserted once again into old roles. My sister, certainly reeling from her many difficult circumstances, resorted to old and toxic behaviours in her treatment of me. For my part, I felt caught between what I saw as the emotional and practical needs of her children and my resentment to aspects of my treatment.

This became especially apparent when an older brother and my father visited to consult with her regarding guardianship and estate plans. Old communication patterns emerged, leaving me outside of all conversations about the children or any next steps, despite my substantial caregiving role. Thus, further undermining my mental wellness. Back then, I didn't know how to change what was happening. So, I too resorted to old victim behaviours.

That meant I said nothing to the people who were hurtful but ranted to my husband and friends. I didn't change my availability, but I did try to stay out of the way. I spent too much time on my own and didn't seek out ways to take and enjoy time for myself.

Growing up believing I held little value, the tendency to say yes to whatever was asked of me became my norm. Or, in this case, evaluating a situation and feeling I must take full ownership of making everything better for everyone else. This way of thinking was detrimental in my personal and professional lives. I didn't know until much later that unless you have firm boundaries, people will ask or accept as much of your time and effort as you let them.

This isn't necessarily opportunistic, just someone trying to get done what they need. If you say yes, they cross that task off their list and move on. If you have said yes without pausing to think about it, then you may, within moments, wonder why you agreed.

Have you ever done that? Said yes right away and then regretted it once you stopped to consider the implications?

Having a life and all its pieces—work, family, friends, community, and self—takes time and effort. If all your effort is for others, then you may find the person most sorry is you, as you struggle to fulfill your promises.

Knowing how to set boundaries and communicate them is important to your physical, mental, and spiritual health. You don't have to be sorry for having a life, you just need to make sure you have one. Setting boundaries is the way to do that.

The next time someone asks you for more of your time, consider to whom or for what you are saying yes. Most of us have plenty of obligations. If you are a habitual yes-sayer, then your plate may be overflowing.

This is where self-love comes in. We are all, every one of us, only able to do our best with the knowledge we have at the time. I made the decision to care for my sister and her children because—at that time in my life—it seemed the right decision.

The person I am now is not the person I was then. A lot has happened. A lot of help has been sought and received. A lot of healing has occurred to leave that sad, victim-living woman in the past.

These days, my boundaries are intact, and I am better able to negotiate my needs and still act compassionately.

If you say yes with a clear mind, not being acted upon by the nice girl or guy syndrome, then enjoy yourself. If you are saying no, do it with the self-assurance of your right to do so. Insert a smile where the sorry would go and with confidence and respect, say no.

## Giving and Receiving Is Not a Greater/Lesser Than Equation

Upon my sister's death, well laid plans unraveled. Care of her children was no longer certain, after the named guardians changed their minds. Ultimately, because I knew what it was to grow up feeling on the periphery of a family, we decided to step up and become what those children needed.

When we chose as a family to become their second family and guardians, it meant a radical change in all of our lives. For them, it meant moving away from their familiar, urban setting to one which my niece, in the last years of her mother's life, refused to visit. Declaring as only a young teen can, her absolute disinterest in anything as "boring" as our small town.

Our children, their cousins, faced similar losses and changes. From diminished living space to parental access, it meant a tremendous shift in the relationships within our family.

Death wasn't a new experience for me. However, compounded loss coupled with the change in our family structure, changed the dynamic of our lives. Forever. It also taught me innumerable lessons about who I thought I was, who I felt I needed to be, and about self-love.

To prepare for my niece and nephew to become part of the family, our entire home needed revamping. Our century old farmhouse was perfect for our family of four. Bedrooms for each of our two children and a small office for our home-based business. The addition of two more teenagers was challenging.

It was a foray into de-cluttering on a grand scale. We weren't building on, so we had to make do.

I knew instinctively that the two girls were going to need their own space. Personalities and temperaments aside, they were also two years apart. I knew from sharing a bedroom with my own sister what a relief it was to have my own space once that became possible. Two additional teenagers joining our family of four in an old farmhouse was overwhelming.

Grief is many things, but an energy generator is not one of them. It fogs our thoughts, slows us down, and disconnects us from much of the outside world. Yet, there I was, tasked to make arrangements that would make the best of our circumstances. I didn't know where to start.

As I sat in my office entering bills and responding to emails one day, I received a personal email. It was from a friend, offering to fly out and help me with the task of reorganizing my home. I looked at the email in disbelief. I read it and walked away. I came back, read it again, and walked away once more. It was such a concrete example of the kind of help I needed, but it also seemed fantastically selfish on my part to accept it. Who was I to have her leave her family on my account? Shouldn't I just be able to get my shit together and get this done? I felt shame and anxiety.

On impulse, I wrote a quick email in reply, "Yes please, if you can." I hit send and then immediately wanted to take it back. Wrong, this was wrong. I was a strong, giving person. I was the giver, not the receiver.

I went outside and thought about it more. I wandered through my gardens, walked around the yard, and considered what I had just accepted. I went back into the house, thinking I should email her again and say, "No, couldn't possibly."

When I got back to my computer, she had already replied. It was arranged. She'd be flying out within days.

## Receiving Is a Lesson in Self-Love

The journey into receiving kindness of tangible help and quiet compassion was a lesson to me about self-love and self-worth. I grew and have become more connected to others, because I was able to accept my limitations and accept the help being offered. There is no debt. I don't have to scramble to repay, and there is no lesser than or greater than. Only giving and receiving.

None of us are islands apart from humanity. Modern society may have led us to believe that being capable and strong is about going it alone, but there isn't anything farther from the truth. Having a need is not being needy. Having a need met is not selfish.

One of the many stories that I had to re-craft from that experience was a re-definition of who I was. Kind, yes. Loving, yes. Perfectly nurturing without needs of my own? No, adamantly no.

Since then, I have also contemplated the burden we put on our men. They too have been held to an emotional rack of being strong no matter what. As women, we need to allow our men to ask for help, to be unsure, to look to us to hold the space for their uncertainty.

This was never clearer to me than during my work as a post-partum doula. Men frequently got mixed messages from the women around them. Yes, we want you to be involved, was the verbalized message to the new fathers; who then found themselves either micromanaged or worse, shamed by their lack of knowledge. The result was the very thing neither parent wanted, for the mother to be the primary caregiver and the father to be in a "support" role on the side lines.

I oddly understood this feeling, because in a twist of life experiences, my husband had the greater knowledge of the care of newborns. He was the eldest of six children and had helped care for his infant siblings. I was the second youngest and had no such interactions. Instead of feeling supported and relaxed with a more knowledgeable person around, I felt anxious and ashamed. Had I the option of retreating to the sidelines, I likely would have. However, as the stay-at-home parent, over time I learned the necessary skills to adequately care for our children.

Whenever we face transition, we are reminded that to thrive, none of us can get through life without being on both sides of the giving and receiving equation.

## Pulling Away the Shroud

I think it's fair to say that most of us want to be seen and accepted for who we are. What happens though, as we pull away the shroud? Sometimes people will mutter that they don't recognize who you are or understand your actions.

Change can create blame, and I've had my share of that. Both as the blamer and the "blamee." I blamed when I didn't take responsibility for what was occurring in my life and wanted to put that on someone else. I accepted being blamed when I wasn't standing up for myself and voicing my needs.

If you grow up striving to be "invisible", this attempt to protect yourself creates the perfect conditions to enter an intimate relationship that honors that wish. While you might crave to be noticed, and treated as special, your personal behavior can undermine that desire. Especially when you don't treat yourself that way. If you choose being agreeable and nice by pushing down your own wants and needs, you're likely to find yourself receiving the exact treatment you don't want.

Until you know that you are practicing doormat behaviour, you can't change it. Dysfunction is drawn to dysfunction. That's your kind of normal, so you seek others who think and act in the same way. Even though it causes pain and you wish for it to be different, the old coping mechanisms continue. Lacking appropriate communication skills and boundary setting, it is easy to get swept up into the emotional storm. Everyone feels the effects, and then rather than addressing those feelings, it is pushed back down. By avoiding conflict and not voicing our needs or wants, the potential for changes in behaviour or increased understanding by those involved is missed.

As you might imagine, this does not solve anything. It tends to allow resentment to grow and fester. Over time, as we continue to repeat the pattern, divisions are created. We get wrapped up in stories that carry a double edge—we are flawed, and we are also victims.

Once we begin to acknowledge that what we want isn't matching up to what we are doing, then the long slow process of healing may begin. The path isn't straight, and it isn't without challenges, but one foot in front of the other begins the journey. Often, the beginning of change begins with a very simple question— why.

## One Person and a Mighty Impact

Have you ever heard adults say they don't know what they want to be when they grow up? That was me, for a very long time. I would wonder, why is it that one person could live a successful, happy life and another flounder and never find their thing?

How do you know that the course of work you are pursuing is the right one? There are no guarantees of course, but the clues are usually found as you are growing up. You don't always see it that way, because you are just following your interests.

Over time, I realized that creating a successful life hinges quite significantly on the early acceptance of you as you are, in every dimension of your personality.

However, if you don't have the conversations that you are meant to have with at least one adult, someone who can see what you don't, you wonder. You wonder, and you wander, and you drift.

Parents obviously play a huge role, but not everyone has the benefit of parents who can or choose to give this type of emotional support.

This can stem from a dozen reasons, including their own beliefs about acceptable pursuits or a need to feed their egos and claim a secondary success through their children. It might even be the result of a negative or fear-based idea about a career choice, worried perhaps about the monetary, physical, or emotional strain it might cause.

Sometimes it is because they simply do not understand or accept their child's personality. An introvert born into a family of extroverts, a daughter interested in business, or maybe a son wishing to pursue the arts: any of these might contribute to a parent's lack of understanding.

In addition to the sad result of adults only living a fraction of what they have to offer, are the negative beliefs that develop about who they are as a person. Perhaps they feel flawed in some way. This can result in a mighty struggle to become everything that is possible, often because of a small insistent voice saying, "You are not enough."

One of the best ways to override that path of fractional living is for one person to reach out and connect with a child or teen or yes, even an adult. One person who can see the bright light and acknowledge all that is possible because of the very fact they have taken the time to see.

Imagine the impact you could have on someone's life if you chose to point out the positive qualities that may have been targets for negative comments. Even better, acknowledge the skills you see. Often people who possess those qualities don't recognize them as skills. They may shrug them off as unimportant or believe that others can do them equally well.

It wasn't until my mid-thirties that I began to see that not everyone was as comfortable with writing as I am. When a supervisor at my workplace remarked that she was struggling to write a memo, I was genuinely surprised. It was then that I began to understand and value my ability to write. Since then, I continue to learn and grow, because each project is different and requires something more.

Even though I have been writing stories and poems since I was a child, it wasn't until that moment that I realized that the skill had merit. Imagine if as a youth, I had received positive feedback about what might be possible. Sometimes I still wonder how my life might have been different, if I'd had one person who had encouraged me.

## Words Matter

The labels applied to behaviour work together with the attempts to remodel someone into an acceptable "version" of themselves. Labels can propel us through life or hold us back.

Would you prefer to be called stubborn or persistent? Too sensitive or empathetic? Arrogant or confident? Of course, stubborn, sensitive, and arrogant are challenging behaviours. If they're causing harm to yourself or others, they may need to be modified. They can, however, also be used against someone by becoming a definition and judgment rather than positive traits that provide for a more connected and successful life.

You can make an impact on others, at whatever age, by simply taking the time to voice your appreciation for their skills and personal qualities. It happens so rarely, that when you are the recipient, it can take time to internalize and accept the comment. When you do, when you can accept the positive feedback, it has the potential to set you on a new path.

Children and adults can all use some positive feedback about the qualities they bring into the world. The question is, are you the one who will do it? For others and for yourself?

## The Mind-Body Connection

Once upon a time, the Western world didn't acknowledge the connection between our minds and our bodies. We are now beginning to see and understand how it impacts us; although, there is much yet to learn.

Tell me, how well do you listen? Not to others, but to all the little messages that your emotional and physical body tries to convey to you? Do you, like I did, try to sidestep or ignore it? If we are receiving messages we don't want, then some of us, many of us, attempt to muffle them. To "put a cork in it" and block it all off. Is it any wonder then that the energy shifts from one form to another?

For a long time, I pushed down unwanted feelings and emotions. I wasn't successful at trying to find my way through them, so I chose not to. This ultimately caused me a lot of emotional and physical pain.

While I won't waste time on regret, I will say this: Had I listened, I imagine that I could have side-stepped a herniated disc. At the time, the doctor called it a cumulative injury. He had no idea just how accurate that diagnosis was.

Given my life experience of being bullied within my family, I grew up feeling as if I didn't belong. I then subconsciously chose a mate who was emotionally unavailable to me. Despite knowing this early in the relationship, I kept trying to change something that was unchangeable. My posture reflected my feeling a lack of support, and the contradiction of wishing to simultaneously be seen and be invisible. Unconsciously, I was folding in on myself.

Author Louise Hay described disease as dis-ease and this definition captured my back injury. The disc bulging at the base of my spine radiated pain down my sciatic nerve. The pain was immense. In the space of two years my ease of movement had dwindled to a nearly non-existent state. Unable to work, outings became few and I became extremely isolated. Despite appointments with both traditional and non-traditional health practitioners, my condition worsened. Faced with the possibility of a life of chronic pain, diminished movement and increasing isolation, I began questioning whether life was worth living. All the things which made my life interesting and meaningful were sliding away. This was another dark night of the soul in which I once again was called to ask myself: Who are you and what do you want?

Then, a series of coincidences occurred.

Friends from my spiritual book club invited me to join them for readings from a psychic. I'd had a reading from another psychic, which had helped me come to terms with the unresolved feelings between my older sister and myself. I found peace in a way that I had not to that point been able to achieve. I was curious as to what this reading would offer and so accepted the invitation.

Since I was open to whatever she might be able to tell me, the results were all the more startling. Within the course of the reading, she told me that a close friend's adult child would be in a car accident in the next few weeks. It would be serious, but the injuries would be minimal.

Next, she told me that someone from my past was going to contact me. That this person would have an offer and it was up to me to decide whether I would accept it. I thought this all to be rather "out there" and curious, until...

Until, she looked me square in the face and said, "You're very unhappy in your marriage and have been considering leaving for a long time. You're going to do it, you know you are. You have a lot of support on the other side, you just need to open up to it. They want you to be happy. "

I had told her nothing about myself, although obviously the wedding ring spoke to a marriage. I certainly wasn't acting unhappy nor had I mentioned any discontent, yet here she was, voicing something I'd been skirting around for months.

I left, curious about her reading.

The very next day, I was indeed contacted by someone from my past and yes, they had an offer. One which I wisely declined, suggesting friendship instead. This proved to be a boon as we mutually moved through difficult transitions and our own life challenges. To this day, I am grateful for that friendship.

That same week, a close friend shared that her son had been in a car accident. His truck was totalled, and he was lucky to walk away with a few bruised ribs and a couple of cuts.

Finally, I dared to really look at my marital situation. Indeed, it wasn't just my back that was causing me pain, but my marriage as well. I was very unhappy and yet had not wanted to "give up", to admit failure. I was also very afraid of the consequences in the relationship with my daughter. I knew that there was a real possibility that my decision could sever our already fragile mother-daughter bond.

We had once been close, but upon the change in our household with her cousins, our relationship suffered to the point of breaking. I knew this could be the proverbial last straw but I came to realize that fearing "what if" in my future relationship with her, was harming me in the present.

The disc bulging at the base of my spine radiated pain down my sciatic nerve. The pain was immense. It didn't truly begin to heal until I accepted the changes I knew I needed to make in my life.

In Eastern religion and medicine, the understanding of the mind-body connection has been developed over thousands of years. To this end, they created what is known as the chakras—places within the body in which energy moves and is directly linked to our emotions. Each chakra has a corresponding connection to the main aspects of our lives. If we become blocked by fear about our safety or financial status for example, then our body's energy will be unable to move as it is meant to. For me, the location of the bulging disc, at the bottom of the spine, is connected to the root chakra. This is the area in which we feel connected to the earth, to our family, and to survival: areas that had been compromised during my childhood and later relationships.

I see awakening with pain one snowy February morning as my body's yell for attention. It was a strong message that it was time for me to wake up and choose whether I would heal inside as well as outside.

This began a journey not just in physical recovery, but also of emotional, psychological, and spiritual healing. I reached out to learn how to resolve all the sources of my pain. I found books by physicians, medical "intuitives", and metaphysical lecturers. Each one identified the mind-body connection. Each also helped me understand how my thoughts and feelings are intricately connected. Several wrote from their own lived experiences, others from their willingness to dig deeper in the lives of their patients and finding unexpected results.

Just as the psychic reading had revealed, my unhappiness could be cured, if I was willing to take the steps. Once I finally made the decision and determined that I would deal with all the consequences, whatever they might be, I felt immediately lighter in mind and body.

None of the healing could happen until I resolved the root cause. Are there truths awaiting your acknowledgement? Signals your body and mind are giving you?

While you may find it difficult to put aside the Western view of health, I think you will be fascinated to learn what's been discovered regarding how stress and childhood experiences impact your health. The consequences of over-nurturing others or of denying your emotions are greater than you might imagine. Research from traditional and non-traditional sources continues to expand our understanding of the mind-body connection creating health or disease. Have a look at the resources in the back, and see where you might find some insight and perhaps even solutions for what's ailing you.

# Part Two: Transformation – Reconcile & Renew

# Chapter 6: Who Are You? Reconciling All the Versions of You

**"Often people attempt to live their lives backwards: they try to have more things, or more money in order to do more of what they want so that they will be happier. The way it actually works is the reverse. You must first be who you really are, then, do what you need to do, in order to have what you want."**

**Margaret Young**

As we grow up, we accumulate roles. No longer just son or daughter, we are student, employee, employer, partner, husband, wife, parent, etc. But who are we really? When we strip all that away, who is the person inside?

That's the struggle isn't it? Just who are you or who do you want to be? When you decide there's a better way to live and to feel, you're inviting the potential for an amazing expansion to your personal world. It isn't always easy, especially at the beginning, but it is absolutely worth the effort as you begin to create more and more experiences of happiness and joy.

Before I was ready to dive in and deal with what needed attention, I spent a lot of time playing online games. I chose to be disconnected from my deeper emotions and live in the superficial fake accomplishments of achieving levels of play. It was easier, but it didn't make my life more satisfying.

That might be you, right now. But facing reality and accepting the discomfort of emotions you would sooner ignore is worth it in the long run. Whatever the precipitating cause, be assured that this is not a place you will stay forever. It is a place of opportunity to redefine who you are and how you will live your life. It can, if you choose, be the beginning of discovering the deeper meaning and purpose in your life.

Since life is about connection and relationships, one of the ongoing opportunities arises at the end of a relationship.

When I was working for a non-profit, I had the occasion to meet a woman whose life was changing once again. Our circumstances of meeting were ordinary. She had contacted my workplace to offer a donation of items, but we had to pick them up. Tasked with this, I arrived at her home ready to have the items loaded into my car, upon which I'd then depart for my next work-related activity.

As Karen* brought boxes out and loaded them into my car, we exchanged pleasantries. I commented that she must be moving out and how exhausting that can be. She looked at me, tears filling her eyes. "Yes," she replied. "This is my boyfriend's place, and I don't have room for these things at my new place. I have spent my life accumulating these things, and now I have to give them away. I am moving into smaller and smaller places and losing all my things."

I stood looking at her, a stranger, tears trickled down her face. I had a moment of choice, as we all do. I could have given a quick thank you and done a speedy retreat. Or, I could risk my own vulnerability and stay in the moment, lean into living from the inside and extend it out.

Ten feet apart, I saw a woman who was talking about things but expressing the loss of self. I said, "I just met you, but I would like to give you a hug, would that be okay?"

"Yes," she said quietly. I held her; we hugged, and she cried some more, apologizing as she did so.

My understanding of what it means to take the steps necessary to move one's life forward gave me the words that were meant for that moment.

"Things aren't us. Our physical space might get smaller, but the world opens in unexpected ways. There's a much bigger life waiting for us than any we imagine right now." We moved apart, and I looked directly into her eyes. "You will be okay; everything you need is inside of you."

## Are You Living the Lottery Mentality?

For many, life is lived with a lottery mentality. All will be well when..., and little effort is made to make the most of what is available at the moment. Little effort, too, to determine for yourself where the riches of your life are.

When I was reflecting on my life a few years ago, I struggled with the disparity between what I had and what was emerging around me. Our unpretentious, rural road was becoming a destination for the wealthy. New estate homes went up, replete with gates, security cameras, and the silent message of those who belonged and those who didn't. For a while, I was internally at odds with what was around me and what my life up to then had been about. Was I a failure? Were my life decisions amounting to a less than equation?

Without turning inward or reflecting on our own measure of success, we risk falling prey to the ideas of others, mindlessly following.

In time, I was able to find the answer. There is no winning when it comes to a life lived. External markers are neither a positive nor negative value of the people residing within. Even though there is much pressure, on both sides, to make them so.

## Living from the Inside Out

When I made the decision to end my marriage I once again had to look at material goods and decide what to keep and what to let go. I was moving from my country home into a tiny apartment. From artwork to books, furniture to clothing, what was really necessary for me to live well and be happy?

Our culture tells us that things are what contain and show the qualities of our lives, the success of it. How many of us hold onto things or behaviors that no longer serve us?

Living from the inside out means fostering the qualities that will always be with us and which carry us through the difficult times and enrich the good times. Compassion, empathy, kindness, and love must each be applied to our own lives to effectively live them out in the world.

Once we do, once we truly believe we are enough as is—quirks and flaws included—we find that things have less importance. The review of my material goods became a shedding of old and the beginning of creating anew. It was as if I was finally embracing the idea of internal self-worth over the external validations of what success looks like.

If we rely on things to define us and be the external validation of our worth, then we will forever be grasping for more. The markers of worldly success change. The timeless qualities of love, compassion, empathy, and kindness exist through all ages and create internal markers from which we can gauge a life well lived.

It's not that material goods don't provide pleasure but rather it's about placing them where they belong. Because as life marches on and people we cherish pass away, we begin to see what truly matters.

As you reflect on where you are and where you want to be, remember to practice self-compassion, kindness, and love. The choices we make at any given time are simply reflections of who we were then. The truths we know of ourselves and others, of how and what we think about the world and our connection to it are like rings on trees. Our lives and choices show how we have grown and what framework of understanding and knowledge we are working from. Some years there's a lot of growth and others less. Regardless, we're going to give ourselves the gift of acceptance.

The initial journey to becoming more of who you wish to be is discarding old unwanted versions. This requires taking time to consider who you are now and thinking about what could be. We're not accustomed to doing that. Even diving into the questions of "Who am I?" "What do I want?" and "What do I like?" can feel overwhelming. If you have been caught up in meeting the needs of everyone else, you may have no idea what your areas of interest are.

## The Starting Line

It begins with taking time for yourself. Yes, time just for you. To reflect. Reflection helps us navigate the deepest part of transition, yet our tendency is to sidestep it. Why? Because it means that we must separate ourselves from distractions and hear our inner voice. To hear this voice requires silence and time alone, two things that are becoming scarce in this age of technology.

If you are curious just how much time you spend online, there are apps to help you see where and how long you are spending checking email and social media. With this awareness, it becomes easier to change your habits in order to spend time in ways that will create more happiness now and in the future.

Plus, for those of you who are people-pleasers it feels a little selfish to call it me time, doesn't it? Or maybe a little bit scary? Instead of the diversions of everyday living, it means purposefully choosing periods of seclusion. This brings clarity and meaning to life experiences. It's also invaluable when creating the next phase of your life. While you don't have control over what happens out there, you do have control over your internal self. To make decisions and to do it well, you are best served by taking a time out and pursuing reflection.

It's not a place to stay, but it is an interior space that you must guard and use so that you are able to fully delve into all aspects of your life.

Reflection is a tool for personal development, where we reject the lure of mindless distract!

## The Value Equation

What do you stand for, or, what won't you stand for?

When we are considering our purpose, we are desperately (sometimes) trying to put together all our "passions" and tie a lovely bow around them. Then say, "Ah ha! Here's my purpose." I don't think it is that simple, nor should it be.

If you are trying to create a life of meaning, it's your values that will help you set the course. In Chapter 1 I asked you to complete the "Wheel of Life" exercise and define your values. Then I asked you to compare your values to what your "Wheel of Life" actually showed. It gave you a starting point to begin asking the big questions. Now, you get to start filling in the fun stuff!

**Excluding values from the plan is a bit like building a house without windows. How will you interact with the world if you've given yourself no way to see either out to it, or into yourself?**

What if, instead of purpose or passion, you chose a vision of what your life might look like? That method frees you up to consider what is important to you, which is another way of saying values. Then, construct a vision around those values. This is likely to bring you round to your interests.

It's possible that you may have considered the values conversation a religious one, but it's not. Integral to deciding how to build your life, values are guidelines of what we will say yes or no to. They help us craft our behaviours, the people we want around us, and the activities we seek out. They really are the decision-making bedrock.

## The Emotion of Decisions Guiding You on Your Path of Purpose

Remember, this is not a personality test. Values are how you choose to be in the world, your guiding principles. Not those of your friend, partner, or career idol. Yours. It's where the phrase "to thine own self be true" comes from. Values, baby, values.

Having any trouble figuring out which ones to choose? Think about recent decisions you have made and see which of these values match up. This is the place to put emotion. Which decisions created a sense of happiness, of pride, or self-fulfillment?

Several years ago, when I was approaching my 50th birthday, I considered how I would like to mark the occasion. I imagined forward to the summer and my day and thought about the who, what and where. Since I had no family other than my adult children and husband in the province, I considered what friends I might like to celebrate with. As I considered the question, I thought of my many friends from around the world. Wouldn't that be something if I could see them, have them with me on my special day?

As I sat in front of my computer, I thought about the possibility of seeing my far-flung friends, people I'd known from my school days who lived across the country and overseas—friends made when I had travelled internationally, the friends who were the family I had chosen.

I was filled with joyful anticipation. I crafted an email, inviting them to come and celebrate my day. Before I hit send, I thought one more time, "Is this what I wanted?" Yes!

I hit send and over the next hours, days and weeks I received reply after reply after reply.

"Yes, yes, yes, can't wait!"

Six months later, on a warm summer evening I was surrounded by friends and immediate family. It is one of the highlights of my life.

The power of defining what I wanted, then taking the action to make it happen, changed the trajectory of my life. One simple decision, "feeling into" what could be, allowed me to begin to change old stories and create new ones.

To be truly successful, to achieve the happiness and fulfillment we are seeking, we need to know what our guideposts are. We are each directed in our lives by what's most important to us.

What's negotiable and what's not?

To discover this for yourself, try making a list of:

1. Your worldly accomplishments—school, work, volunteer—awards or recognition you received
2. Personal accomplishments—what you're proud of achieving or doing
3. Friendships and what you value in them
4. When you have felt let down by a person or an organization
5. When you have been encouraged by actions or words

Once you have completed this, use the Values List in the appendix to see which values apply to you. This will help you find your true north, the foundation upon which you want to create the rest of your life. Also in play in this discovery process is extracting the wisdom of the ages. This can be found through books, nature, the pursuit of creative expression, and talking with those willing to explore areas of introspection.

Within this time of reflection, you are choosing your responsibility in the creation of your life as it is right now. If you want something different (and you do, don't you?), then you must reflect on what areas you feel need a new life map.

## Using Journal Writing for Reflection and Motivation

On this journey of crafting a life of joy, I have asked you to gather information, begin thinking about what you want and feel into what the future could be. Having all that swirl around in your head can be overwhelming, which is why using a journal to record those thoughts, hopes and dreams is powerful.

Much more than a diary, your journal is a safe place to get down on paper your daily thoughts and reflections. A journal helps you wade through all the information you are acquiring and pull it into the fold of consciousness.

Author Julia Cameron's preferred timing is at the start of the day. She refers to the practice of "morning pages" as a means of releasing everyday thoughts to free up the space for more creative and productive thinking later. It's not meant as the start of the next great novel, it is simply a means of emptying yourself, so you can fill yourself in other ways.

Don't fret if you believe this is best suited to "writers." It's just another means of getting in touch with yourself and the thoughts that swirl through your mind. It can relieve tension. It's also a great way to begin getting in touch with who you are.

This is a private and personal document not meant to be shared. It allows you the freedom for total honesty without the constraints of societal, cultural or relationship rules. You don't have to be polite and you don't even have to worry about your spelling or grammar. Get your thoughts and emotions down, and then when you are ready, turn those same thoughts on their heads and consider what you have learned.

Self-reflection and self-awareness are the hallmarks of self-leadership. With time and maturity your ability to choose to find the value of your discontent can be found. What lessons are within your experiences? To become truly responsible for your life, accept the chance to review all areas and think about where and what you will change as you move forward.

Every life-changing event has both a dark and a light side. The dark side is felt as remorse and regret, anger, sadness, and even grief. We feel it because we know that the person we were is shifting, and we don't know into what or how this will affect our presence in the world.

Nevertheless, we are moving forward and doing so means discarding ideas and beliefs that no longer serve us. The light side is the new self that emerges, an awakening and stirring of pieces that may have been dormant. A sparkle in the eye, ready laughter, and even a spring in the step are all signs of successful movement through the unknown to this new place in your life.

Each of us will experience life obstacles and disappointments.

We can choose to use them or try to ignore them and go on with life as it existed before. In the event you are willing to use and not hide from them, remember the following: While you may traverse much of the darkness on your own, you have at hand the tool of reflection and a few souls willing to join you for a portion of your trip.

The important changes you make occur inside. Stay the course and know that you are exactly where you are meant to be.

In time, you will find that your new you is more than capable of creating the next chapter.

## What's Your Type?

When you've grown up feeling as if you are inherently flawed, you don't look too far for other information. I had no idea that my preferences for social gatherings, work styles, and relationships stemmed from being an introvert. This is a personality type, not a character flaw.

Susan Cain's brilliant book, Quiet: The Power of Introverts in a World That Can't Stop Talking, led me to understand who I am. Rather than believing I was a singular and odd soul, Cain's book helped me see I was part of a much larger group.

Cain's book sheds light on the reasons that introverts act as they do, what they need to be happy and enjoy their lives. Within her book, I discovered an explanation for pieces of myself that, in the past, I had to defend. Things like turning down social engagements when I felt my energy was low, requiring quiet when focusing on tasks, or why I wanted time to review information before giving an opinion. And finally, why, when at a social function, I was more likely in the corner with a few people than trying to speak to every person in the room.

Reading Cain's book, or any other book for that matter, gives us the chance to see ourselves or others in a new light. What would this mean for yourself or for those you are in relationships with? Does it help you better define and express what it is that you need? The North American culture tends to celebrate extroversion and when you don't fit that model, it is easy to feel judged.

The introverts in your life are likely to turn down social engagements more often, require time alone to recharge and process the interactions and conversations. It's a mental inhalation/exhalation, allowing the body and mind to relax.

Michelle Obama, in her book Becoming, shares that Barack is an introvert. Given a politician's schedule, it is hard for me to imagine how he managed to juggle the demands and his needs. Apparently, one way he accomplished this was by creating a small space to call his own, regardless of where they were. He needed a place to spread out his books, papers and notebooks and close the door as needed. I can totally relate to that. Were you an introvert in a family of extroverts? Or perhaps surrounded by extroverts at work? Knowing what you need, whatever your type and expressing those needs without concerns about acceptance or judgment is the hallmark of healthy relationships. Without that knowledge of self or others, judgments and stories can be created about behaviour, leading to walls which inhibit understanding.

I think there is a general misperception that everyone in the public eye is an extrovert, but more likely, like me, they have found ways to recharge. To an extrovert, no doubt an introvert's actions might seem unfriendly or a display of poor social skills. Of course, neither is true.

Many introverts especially enjoy the opportunity to spend more time conversing with a few people at a deeper level, rather than many at the surface level.

Where extroverts thrive on more people, more energy, and quick decisions, introverts look for pacing and opportunities to be alone.

Extroverts have full calendars. They're happy to accept invitations, join in the post-work fun, and attend social events. They re-energize from the company of those present. Too much time alone, and they'll be putting out a call to see who is free.

Introversion and extroversion are, of course, on a spectrum. It's not all-or-nothing. Many introverts have learned how to succeed within the parameters of the extroverted work culture, and many extroverts know when they'd benefit from some down time.

This type of information is important as you move forward. Both in understanding what you need so you can explain it to others and in ensuring that your needs are met by working with others.

## To Thine Own Self Be True – Your Most Important Relationship

In order to maintain your most important relationship, where you honour the phrase "to thine own self be true," you must really know what is true for you. Recently, I had one of those ah-ha moments, and it both amused and informed me. It made so much sense that I wondered why I hadn't put it together sooner.

Once upon a time, as a young single woman, I was playing cards with a friend. Growing bored, we decided to make a bet. The loser had to do a chore for the winner. I have no idea what I agreed to do if I lost, but as the winner I do recall that my friend had to clean my apartment. She did a great job, every surface shone, and nothing was out-of-place. It was very nice and unlike my usual style.

Part two of the story is where this set of circumstances set the foundation for years of misunderstandings, upset, and arguments. Picture my new boyfriend coming to visit. He looks around, appreciates the very tidy and clean apartment, and draws the silent conclusion that this is the way I always live, that it's my way of being. It wasn't and isn't.

When I write, it's possible for there to be a sink full of dirty dishes, a floor that needs sweeping, and clothes to be put away. I'm very comfortable leaving those chores until the writing is done. It doesn't weigh on me. I have come to understand that for some, and I was married to one of them for twenty-nine years, it's the same sensation as fingernails down a chalkboard. Intolerable.

## The Healthiest Relationships Start with Self-understanding and Acceptance

Why does this matter? Because if we don't know, understand, and accept ourselves, we can hardly begin to form healthy, functioning relationships with others. If the way I am is very different from the way you are, we either find a middle ground and negotiate the differences, or we limit the relationship.

Self-reflection allows us to unravel what we think we know about ourselves, to examine different situations and see our part in them. Not with the inner critic shouting in your ears, but as the means of creating a kinder and more loving relationship with yourself. For any relationship to really succeed, you need to know who you are: what matters, what doesn't, and what's negotiable.

On this journey of me, myself, and I, you are best served to understand yourself in and out of a relationship. Each introspection helps to uncover what's hidden from your view and the missing pieces you want or need to develop.

## Self-discovery Allows You to Live Authentically

The period of self-discovery is perhaps the biggest gift you can give yourself. You become freer to be yourself by understanding the how, why, and when you've let yourself down by not being true to yourself. Over time, you can see all the ways in which you can emerge as the best version of yourself.

When we begin to take responsibility for ourselves and for our needs, it helps us to define what we need. One of the key areas is learning how to interpret expressions of love and appreciation.

Have you ever received a gift from your partner and wondered what they were thinking? Or maybe you spent hours researching the best deal for them on an item they were thinking of buying and the response was…lackluster?

Trouble arises in how people interpret and express love. We tend to work from our own ideas of what constitutes expressions of our deepest feelings. We learn at home, within our families, how Mom and Dad do things, or how they interact with us.

We are often unaware that there is more than one way to show affection. This is unfortunate because misinterpretation can lead to judgment and a movement away from fostering the love we feel.

## The Languages of Love

Author and marriage counselor, Dr. Gary Chapman, brings forward the idea of the "5 Languages of Love": words of affirmation, acts of service, receiving gifts, time together, and physical touch. He suggests that each of us has primary ways of understanding these expressions of love.

I hadn't really thought of that before. It certainly helped me understand the times when I've felt really loved and when I've felt let down. It also helped me realize when my partner was expressing love as he knew it and the hurt he must have felt when it went unacknowledged.

For instance, I really care about time together and physical touch, but less so about gifts or acts of service, such as my car being washed. I notice it, but I don't feel bathed in the love of someone. Take time out of your day though, do something with me, and that's special indeed.

We tend to give what we want and can feel rejected or judged if that doesn't happen to match up with what our partner is looking for, or what it is that we want. I now have a very important tool in not just getting what I need, but also in stepping up to make the effort for those I love in the ways that fill their hearts.

Presumably, you want your relationship to thrive. The best way of doing so is to acknowledge what it is you're seeking and ask what your loved one needs. You might be surprised.

## Re-write Your Love Stories

Once you know the ways in which your loved ones feel cherished then you can re-write some of the stories you may have created. Stories which impact your feelings about how much you are cared for or loved. Release the hurt, judgment, and sadness; re-kindle appreciation, love, and kindness. That seems like an extraordinary outcome.

As you approach the rest of your life, explore these expressions of love. What is it that speaks to your heart? What speaks to those you care about? Once you know, act and enjoy the results.

Relationships, old and new, will benefit from this self-knowledge. All any of us can do, in fact what we must do, is be true to ourselves. When we are, we have so much to offer the world.

## Values, Religion, and Spirituality

Somewhere along the way, as you try to determine your identity and values, you are likely to find yourself questioning God, organized religion, and spirituality.

You may find your faith and connection deepening in your established beliefs, or you may find that there is a complete rupture. Regardless, you won't get there without some deep soul searching.

Defining our values isn't an aimless exercise; its impacts are far-reaching: from job to relationship to faith. This became very clear to me as I simultaneously dealt with my mother's spiralling descent into alcoholism, and the emerging scandal of the Catholic Church and child-abuse perpetrated by some of their priests.

Raised Catholic, I'd been steeped in a history of service and inherent worth defined by gender. I struggled with this as I parented my two children. I had never identified as a feminist, even though my mother's passionate activism was a clear role model. I found however, as parenting brought my own values to the forefront, that my unquestioning acceptance as a child was now being challenged.

It is one of the rites of passage to becoming fully responsible for your life.

While it is our inherent responsibility to define our values and teach them to our children as a guidance system, there comes a time when they must define and choose their own.

When the scandals of child sexual abuse came to light, I felt a sense of betrayal by the lack of responsibility the leaders chose to accept. I realized then, how much I care about the integrity of words and actions. I cannot follow those who choose to lead in the manner of "do as I say, not as I do."

Perhaps my response was intensified by the bullying I experienced, but whatever the cause, I realized that the church which had been so closely tied to my identity was no longer a good fit.

Once again, the sands of my foundation shifted. Who else was I or could I be, without those teachings from my childhood?

When you have belonged to something that is a part of your identity, choosing to leave it behind creates a gap, a hole you look to fill. The journey of self-development requires both discarding and creating. It is a duality of loss and creation.

From a psychological perspective, we are wired for connectivity, but most of us also seek a connection to something greater than ourselves. When we discard one belief system or identity, we then often find ourselves asking, "Who or what do I believe?"

As we dig deeper into creating our truth and the essence of our lives, we become seekers of meaning and connection.

We prepare ourselves for the evolution of self.

## Assembly Required

Have you ever bought an item that needed to be assembled? It may be daunting, but at least there's a manual to show what the item is supposed to look like when done. When we decide that the time has come to move forward, the lack of a manual can be a little scary, and yet oddly refreshing too.

A decision to end a relationship requires conscious selection of what to keep and what to let go. It requires disassembly.

To take apart, to break into pieces, to separate. It's a crucial part of the journey. There are challenging moments, hours, and, yes, even days; but the forward movement is a conscious one.

I vividly recall my first morning in my tiny apartment following the move out of my marital home. It was the smallest space I'd lived in since my days in university. Sitting in my little kitchen, radio playing in the background, I fairly beamed with joy. In the process of letting go of many material goods, I'd come to appreciate how much the forward movement enhanced my life. I have fewer things—part of the disassembly required.

What I've found, recovered, and reassembled are parts of myself I hadn't realized were MIA. It was the lack of action and forward movement that caused some of the qualities to go missing. Things like confidence, self-assurance, and desire.

I know I'm not the only one who allows that to happen. Over-dependence on another, a limited view of how to live life, and becoming mired in patterns of behaviour keep us stuck and small.

I now know that what I make of my life is up to me. I define my boundaries. I accept or put aside the things, people, and experiences that will either enhance my life or put me back into neutral.

## Push Past Self-limiting Patterns

Looking forward—moving forward—means pushing past self-limiting patterns and peeking into a new vision of what could be. Ever the optimist, I am planning a bigger life. Creating it will require determination, persistence, and consistency. The more I do, well, the more I do.

Our lives—our very selves—can appear as a jumble of unrelated parts, with no directions available. It is worth the disassembly and reassembly. Interestingly, each action brings unexpected new versions of ourselves that we hadn't realized were possible.

Ending my marriage of twenty-nine years was a decided challenge. But once I began the process, I found the forward movement of a long-delayed decision to be invigorating. There were many areas to attend to, but the relief in finally letting go of limiting and negative behaviours was the wind beneath my wings.

I've discovered that I can indeed rock some new, out-there eyewear and be more comfortable with my feminine side. I'm also tougher than I was led to believe. I'm not likely to fold even when the weight of the world feels solidly on my shoulders.

# Chapter 7: Finding Your Way

**"The center that I cannot find is known to my unconscious mind."**

**W. H. Auden**

If we accept that life is change, then it follows that life is also transition. When people say they don't like change, I believe it's the transition they don't like.

Change has a before and after. Caterpillar, butterfly. Seed, flower. Teenager, adult. Transition is difficult. It is an emotionally (and perhaps physically) painful process of becoming or creating something new. It is brutally hard work that makes you wonder if you can do it.

Transition pushes us down a road that has no end in sight. Why do we do it? Because not doing so is even more painful.

My experiences of transition have taken me from who I was or thought I was to someplace and someone new. I am challenged at every turn to uphold my sense of self and often my values. Sometimes it has felt rough, sore, and relentless. Especially in the middle space, where we are too far along to go back, but unable to see what might be ahead.

As a new parent I struggled through the transition of a change of roles from individual to motherhood I was one of those parents who looked at my infant and felt no immediate emotional connection (not uncommon according to research, but not widely discussed either). Who I thought I was and what I could cope with, compounded by a baby with colic, and yes, that messy middle space emerged. It wasn't all sunshine and roses and just like sandpaper on a piece of wood, I experienced a sanding down which brought out the inner beauty waiting to be discovered.

Every difficult experience has taken me into the messy middle ground, where at different points I long to curl into a ball and say, "Enough, enough!" Experience doesn't give us a hall pass, but it can provide us with at least a nugget of faith that we can move through the current challenge and emerge transformed. I can say, with confidence, that if you are willing to stay open to the pain, look inside and into the uncertainty, you won't be the same person who began the journey.

Transitions rarely result in fanfare, except for what you feel inside. Take heart, because that's where you can continue to expand your life into a greater and wider realm than what you now imagine.

## Creating Your “My Time” Chapter

Are you creating the next phase of your life? Reflection is a solo activity that brings clarity and meaning to life experiences. The chapter of my time is surfacing more as people contend with empty nests, relationship changes, job loss, retirement, or health challenges. Change surrounds us. Ready or not, decisions must be made. We don’t have control over what happens out there, but we do have control of our internal selves. To make decisions and to do it well, we are best served by taking a time out and pursuing reflection.

Within this time of change, we must include our responsibility in the creation of our lives as they are right now. If we want something different, then we must reflect on what areas we feel need new life maps. In accepting full responsibility for our lives and our choices, we also need to include self-compassion, kindness, and love. The choices we make are reflections of who we are at any given time. The truths we know of ourselves and others, of how and what we think about the world and our connection to it.

Lately, I have participated in or heard conversations of people attempting to determine how to build the next chapter—the my time chapter—of their lives. Most have spent their lives in the service of others, through work, to family (extended or otherwise), and to their communities. Now, they are attempting to discover and uncover the areas that build satisfaction and energy into their daily lives. No longer satisfied with what has been, they are ready to create a focused approach. A life which meets more of their needs than the earlier status quo.

## Why Reflect?

Reflection gives the opportunity to redefine who you are and how you will live your life. It helps you navigate the deepest part of transition and yet the tendency is to side step it. Why? Because it means that we must separate ourselves from distractions and hear our inner voices. To hear this voice requires silence and time alone, two things that are becoming scarce in this age of technology. Instead of the diversions of everyday living, getting the greatest benefit from this tool means purposefully choosing periods of seclusion. Choosing reflection ushers in a time of information and resource gathering, as well as taking opportunities for conversations with people unafraid to talk about the deeper aspects of life. The inner space is not a place to stay, but we must guard it so that we are able to fully delve into all aspects of our lives.

True transition and life-altering changes have a beginning, middle, and end. It is in the middle where it is possible to feel most adrift. Why? Because we are in uncharted waters with few who will meet us there. Nevertheless, we must accept the discomfort of emotions we would sooner ignore.

Have you ever witnessed the abandonment of people who have experienced the loss of someone close to them? In part it is because while your life has changed, theirs has not. While you find your way in your new normal, they are continuing to live their lives as they exist. Then, there are those people so uncomfortable with death that they choose to distance themselves in the fear of saying the wrong thing. Little do they know that there is no perfect thing to say, rather it is the act of showing up and being in the space with you that is comforting.

Reflection is a tool for personal development where we reject the lure of mindless distractions. Instead, we accept the discomfort of emotions we would sooner ignore. Whatever the precipitating cause, be assured that this is not a place you will stay forever. It is a place of opportunity to redefine who you are and how you will live your life.

Being in transition is being in a state of decision-making. It's the process of trying to make sense of a series of choices appearing to make no sense at all and which we know are going to result in change.

At one time, in the not too distant past, there was a gaping hole where interest, talent and purpose should have resided and didn't. I'd lost them because I'd never nurtured them or been taught how they could coincide with everyday living.

Based on my work with others also trying to transition from "Is this it?" to "This is it!" it's not such an uncommon problem. The first part of the journey is a rediscovery of yourself. The second is how to fit it all together without going into overwhelm and shutting down.

Even when there are a lot of great choices, choosing the what, when and why enhances our overall plans for the directions we want to take. Saying no doesn't mean no never, it can simply be, no; not now.

## Self-leadership Is the Key to Transition

The old saying "when the going gets tough, the tough get going" is meant to be motivational. But I always felt on the outside of the statement. In part because I felt it was a more masculine phrase, but also because for a long time, I didn't feel very tough. What I did feel was aimless, directionless, and lonely.

That was back in my twenties, and my life felt stalled.

I'd graduated from university, spent a remarkable year with the international group Up with People, and then found myself alone and without any idea of what might be next. Instead of crafting a vision of possibilities from that year of travel, I felt adrift.

Up until then, the path had been laid out for me: expectations about schooling and then beginning work of some sort. I'd chosen the year of travel, but it hadn't brought me any closer to choosing a direction or creating a vision for my life.

My friends were all moving towards big career goals. I was still trying to figure out what I wanted to be when I grew up. Does that sound familiar? Perhaps you've said it yourself, half-joking. But being unable to connect the dots of your skills and interests is no joke.

## Loss of Personal Vision, Loss of Self-leadership

Self-leadership is the answer to the dilemma, but how does one develop such a thing? Is it taught or is it intrinsic? Nature or nurture? I think the answer is all of the above.

What I do know is that leadership can be squeezed out of you. It's possible to teach someone they have no value and won't amount to much. That is a means to quashing any ability to create a life of purpose. Just ask anyone who has been in an abusive relationship.

It also happens to children and teens who have been bullied.

My interests got a thumbs down from my family: involvement with the family business to pursuing a stage career to considering teaching or social work. I kept looking for external validation and approval and instead was met with criticism, negativity, or indifference. This isn't a recipe for success.

## Start with What You Enjoy

If self-leadership pivots on the ability to formulate a vision for your life, how do you overcome the idea that what you have to offer is neither special nor important? I believe you start with what you enjoy, add more of it into your life, and then look for how it can benefit others.

How does this help someone who is trying to build his or her life? By creating a vision and a goal.

You become a part of something larger than yourself. Connection to others, being a member of a community and using your skills are all ways to build up your own sense of value while bringing value to others. There are few things more fulfilling than doing something you enjoy and then finding ways to make it of value to others.

## A Great Vision Includes Benefits to Others

When we're trying to formulate a vision, it starts with a question: "What do I want?" There is a second question that helps you define the answer: "How can what I want to achieve be a benefit to others?" The path of determining what you want doesn't necessarily reveal itself all at once. It's why taking steps to begin following an interest will help you decide some of those finer points.

Consider, for example, an interest in sewing (or podcasting or fly fishing).

You've done a few projects on your own. Then you see that a local shop is providing classes. You're interested and sign up. Over the span of the course, you get to know others and begin hearing about other events and courses. Then you hear about a new project for people in a senior's residence; they're looking for volunteers to assist. Signing up, you get to know a few people from the original group better as well as some amazing seniors.

Every week, you look forward to getting together with your community. Soon, you begin to think about some outreach projects that would bring this skill to a larger population. As you talk it up with a few others, you decide to form a committee. You find yourself busier and more connected than you'd imagined.

## Personal Leadership is a Process, Not a Destination

Is this your job? No. Will it be? Who knows?

The point is that through the process you've come to understand that not only can you sew (run a podcast or create fly fishing ties), you also have an ability to connect with people.

The benefits are numerous. First, you've allowed yourself to do something you enjoy. Then, you put yourself a little further into the world. Finally, you set out a goal to help someone else and were able to achieve it. These are all a part of the process of creating your vision.

Within the process of self-leadership is coming to understand that we are all connected and overriding any messages of aloneness. We are not alone. Not at work, not in our communities, and not in the world. Choosing and following a path gives you the gift of new experiences, new connections, and new opportunities. Even if those opportunities are not immediately obvious.

## Vision, Personal Power, and Success

It's hard to be taught that you have no worth. It's equally hard to feel that you can't solve problems as they arise. If you feel that way, you are unlikely to pursue your dreams. When uncertainty and overwhelm strikes, you are even less likely to attempt what seems a grand dream.

Trying to figure out everything before you get going absolutely pushes you to overwhelm. Fear can keep you from starting, because you are aware of how much you don't know, forgetting that you likely know enough to get started and can exercise your ability to learn what you don't.

What I've learned in the process of writing this book is that it is enough to focus on the writing. There are many steps to come, likely ones I am not aware of, but first the book must be written.

The many ways we get in our own way, by trying to think it all through beforehand, was amusingly pointed out by a child of seven.

I was facilitating one of my signature in person 100% Events and a woman shared that she would like to create a journal with inspiring quotes but was feeling "stuck". As it happened the host's child was there and when asked what to do, she quite seriously answered the question. "Take sheets of paper, put them together with a stapler and write the quotes on each piece." In other words: Don't overthink it, just start.

By choosing to begin and trusting that you can find the support and knowledge you need along the way, you build your sense of self-worth and belief that you are able to handle whatever challenges arise. This is known as self-efficacy and is one of the pillars of self-leadership.

Without self-worth and self-efficacy, you lose sight of your internal vision of what your life could be and what you can accomplish. That loss compounds to a lack of personal power to make change for yourself or others. Overcoming this narrow and limiting view is very liberating.

Self-leadership is not a one-shot deal. It's an ongoing journey into setting a course, travelling it, and correcting and expanding as time goes on. Just because you are unsure now, doesn't mean that you will always be. Give yourself the gift of starting down a path, of choosing what you want, and then believing in yourself to handle what comes up along the way.

If you feel stuck, don't have a vision, or are trying to figure out what you want to be when you grow up, know you aren't alone. If you need help in moving your life ahead, contact me. I can help. I've been there.

While I was living my semi-life during my back-injury days, I found that writing out what I wanted, how I would spend my time once my back healed, was helpful. It was a positive, forward-thinking exercise which kept me hopeful about life's possibilities.

I gifted myself this exercise several times because I didn't know the future of my back and healing. I was determined not to live in chronic pain, and so the journal kept me hopeful. Now it's your turn; grab your journal and complete the following statements:

If I had more time, I would:

If I had more courage, I would:

If I had more money, I would:

Let it flow, no self-editing and logic. Let your inner self speak to you. Let it help you find the path you wish to travel.

Next it's time to decipher what you want less of. Once again, let it flow. Be absolutely honest. What you see here will help you decide what your overall picture could look like.

Try these to get you started:

Less time doing:

Less money spent on:

Less doubt about:

Your answers, especially if you go with the first things that come up, are powerful. This is your inner voice, your knowing and it is from here that you can create.

Once answered, tuck them away and pull them out as you begin to create your “my time” chapter.

# Chapter 8 – Stepping Into Your Life

## Becoming the Change You Wish To See

**"Time and tide wait for no man."**

**Geoffrey Chaucer**

We may wish that time waited, especially if we are faced with the end of something we've enjoyed. Or, if we fear what the end will bring. Life has a way of rolling forward, whether we want it to or not. Jobs, circumstances and even people come and go in our lives. Some are location moves, others are relationship changes and yes, some are due to the final passing in which those closest to us are no longer of this world.

Yet, have you discovered that when you accept that all things pass into yesterday, what you do today, matters?

This might be as simple as telling someone you appreciate them, or it might be signing up for a course you are interested in or beginning a new fitness regimen.

If neither time nor tide wait, why do you?

## The Tides of Change Are Never Stalled, Only Our Responses to Them

Is the lottery mentality keeping you on the sidelines? Are you waiting for the perfect moment? To have all the answers or exactly the right amount of money, skills or certainty? If you are, consider that your life may be stalled.

To live a life of continued meaning, you must continue to make choices that move you forward. Knowing, as you do, that life is change, what circumstances are you willing to acknowledge that are ready for some fresh life?

It takes some courage to review what was and plan for what's next.

All of us have something that sits at the back of our minds, in our hearts. In the very deepest parts of ourselves that we rarely or never share with others.

When I was sidelined with that back injury five years ago, the courage question circled my brain. If my back healed (and for a while I wasn't certain it would), what would I want to be doing with my life? What would change; how might I change?

## Your Soul Is Yearning for You to Answer Its Call. Will You?

Please consider asking yourself the courage question and allow what bubbles up to see some light. Give yourself the chance to think about and feel what those ideas bring to you. Pleasure? Interest? Curiosity? Energy?

Beginning to act on those bubbles of inner promptings, moves you closer to making the changes that your soul is yearning for. One decision, one step towards what those callings are, marks the beginning of your next grand adventure.

It is the interior shifts of your journey which move you forward. Not away from what was, but rather adding to the tapestry of your life.

If time and tide wait for no one, are you trying to do the impossible by holding onto your yesterdays?

## Self-leadership Is What Keeps You Out of a Stalled Position

Self-leadership is the conscious choice to take control of your life; when you choose to take responsibility and ride the tides of change rather than drift on them.

So, I'm asking you again. Are you waiting for everything to be perfect? For the "t's" to be crossed and the “i’s” to be dotted? Or are you willing to answer your soul’s calling? Knowing that only some of the journey will be revealed to you, while the rest will come as you continue to step forward into your future?

While it may feel uncomfortable, not knowing where your decisions will take you, it becomes easier over time. No doubt you will find all the other emotions that come with choosing your next steps outweighing the uncertainty of knowing all the possible outcomes.

## From Stalled to Creating New Stories

Five years ago, I wrote down: start a business, write a book, travel.

As you may be aware, I am mid-stream in creating all those and so much more. Prior to finding the courage to set down my path, to choose what came next, my life had indeed stalled. It took a back injury and time to reflect on what I really wanted, to get it going again.

What does it feel like, those first steps into creating change for yourself? Of choosing a course of action and deciding that you are ready to create and create again? Exciting and maybe a little bit scary too? If that’s the case, you are on the right road my friend, because every time I’ve chosen to move on a goal that seems just a little bigger than I'm ready for, I feel both of those things.

## Blossoming Occurs as a Result of the Choices You Make

Imagine, if you were completely uprooted and on your own once again? What would that mean for you? How would you fill your time? What activities and people would you choose? Just like a cactus waiting to bloom, the choices you make provide the nourishment needed to make it possible.

Endings are always challenging, because it requires you to say goodbye: goodbye to people, places and in some cases, plans for the future. Calling an end to my marriage meant leaving a home I loved, surrounded by nature and quiet and many memories. However, we are not meant to live in yesterday, to quit planting seeds of possibility, to quit stretching our roots and branches. If I were to grow, it meant moving on.

For my part, it meant taking on the challenge of being single in a couples' world. I sought new ways of engaging with the world and found the many offerings of city living. By attending lectures and groups, the idea of writing a blog began to seem more possible, more exciting and yes, a little scary.

Were there times of loneliness, fear and uncertainty? Yes, of course. But also, friendship, wonder, curiosity and laughter. Life isn't, or shouldn't be, just one flavour.

## Blossoming Happiness

Your endings don't need to be as big as mine. In fact, it might be as simple as choosing to try one new thing alone, or with your partner. To challenge yourself with changing your evening or weekend pattern. It could even mean deciding to take on something new at work. Sign up for a committee or seek out a mentor if you are interested in growing into a new position.

Novelty is important to our happiness and by including it in your life, you nourish your whole self—body, mind and soul. Throw out old limiting ideas of what you think is possible and begin to stretch into something new. Setting in motion the chance for buds to set and blossoms to occur.

For your life to blossom, you only need to put in the time and patience to make it so.

Is it ever too late to make those changes? Some people certainly think "that boat has sailed." Then you meet someone like my former neighbor.

Diagnosed with terminal cancer, all possible treatments done, *Alice continues to make decisions based on what she wants now and with whatever future remains. While Alice knows she is on a faster track to the end than the rest of us, she refuses to lie down and wait. Instead, she stubbornly lives. Alice walks the talk by continuing to live the mantra she taught her daughters: "Don't wait for someone else to create the life you want."

Stubbornly live. There is power in that, don't you think? Aren't there times when we would all, at one point or another just...settle? Accept "what is" without questioning "what else"? Would you, if the end was in sight, shrug and say, "Too late now"?

## Forget "What Is" and Ask "What Else?"

Accepting "what is", is a mistake that often happens as a result of sliding into a pattern, without any real thought to when or why it started. Creating goals, envisioning our lives over the long-term slides to the back of our decision-making and we accept our lives as "just the way things are."

Take for instance your love relationship. Is it unsatisfying? If so, why is it? What exactly is missing for you? Is it something you had and it slipped away with the daily demands of getting things done? There are few things lonelier than being in the same room with someone and feeling as if there is a Grand Canyon of space between you.

Stubbornly living challenges the current state of your life and pushes through what others might see as obstacles. If it had a voice, it might well say, “Move over; there’s a whole lot more for me to do yet!” A life review doesn’t need to come with a diagnosis of a serious health concern. In fact, it can happen as part of an ongoing process.

Remember the “Wheel of Life” exercise? This is a great opportunity to pull it out again and review the areas needing attention. Choose one area and let your imagination come and play. Envision what your life would look like if that one area scored more highly. Yes, I know, that damn reflection again!

## Own Your Life. Show Up

Stubbornly living demands that you sit up and take stock. Going back to your relationships, intimate or otherwise, there are important aspects for your consideration. With journal in hand, consider these questions:

If you have a relationship that is less than what you want, what circumstances changed? Something in your life, or in theirs? What interests do you share and do those interests still exist? If not, are you willing to search out alternatives or a new version of the old interest?

If your long-term intimate relationship is the one in question, what has changed? Has it dwindled from shared experiences and love-mate to that of housemate? Do you feel that you know everything there is to know about them? When is the last time you tried something new together?

If you are willing to get out of your own way, chances are good that surprises still await. Put aside the notion that your choices are limited and instead, begin reaching for what is possible.

Sometimes it is as simple as changing routines; other times it is about asking yourself whether the relationship needs more attention. Are there conversations that have been left, that need to occur? Or, have you failed to grow your own life and the effects are now being felt with others? Start thinking about what has stirred your curiosity and then take a chance; have the conversation.

And if you are single, your life is also ripe for examination and change. Ask yourself these questions as you look to ignite your life:

Is there something you haven't done because of time or money?

Have you delayed following through on an interest because you don't want to do it alone?

While real, these obstacles are best viewed as challenges. Don't give them more weight than they deserve or make them excuses for not achieving what you want.

When you decide what is important to you and what you want, you have found the springboard to achieving it.

Time, money or any of the other limitations you feel you have can be solved with a willingness of spirit. While I was employed and writing my blog, I got up a couple of hours earlier each morning. While not an early riser by nature, it was the easiest time for me to fit in the writing. I am certainly not the first person to adjust my life to follow through on my goals.

In her book Becoming, Michelle Obama reflects on her days of living a single-parent lifestyle while Barack worked in another city. She valued the benefits of fitness so chose to get up at 4:30 a.m. to fit in her early morning workout. She asked her mother to come and be with her children so she could accomplish this. I imagine it meant long days, but she found a way around the obstacle.

Likewise, Canadian businesswoman and single mother, Arlene Dickinson problem-solved by taking her young children to work when there were no other options. She did what she had to and her children adjusted to the circumstances. Too often, we shortchange ourselves by underestimating what is possible from ourselves or others in our lives.

Obstacles are real, but when your desire to achieve a happier and more fulfilled life is stronger than your current situation, you may be surprised by your ingenuity in finding answers to the problem. Neither of those women would likely say those years or solutions were easy, but they chose to fulfill their commitments to themselves and to their work.

Whether it is money, time or other resources, it is not always easy, but there is almost always a way around, through or over every obstacle that comes your way.

## Have You Cast Yourself into a Limited Role?

Have you become stuck seeing yourself as a certain type of person who does or does not do certain things? If so, why and where did that image come from? Have you held yourself back, pushed down interests because of external messages about what is acceptable, or worth your time? What areas of your life are waiting for you to stretch or expand? Are there ideas worth challenging? What messages have you received and accepted as being truth, without ever really looking at them?

For a long time, I gave up many expressions of my feminine side. Some were due to my old childhood stories while others came about in my marriage. Since dysfunction is attracted to dysfunction, I found a partner who was willing to support my self-view. His personal insecurities danced with mine and together we created a story which kept me small in expressions of self personally and professionally. Remember, the universe answers what we put out to it. As long as I was giving a vibrational message of "not good enough," then that was the very kind of partner I attracted.

Once I decided to embrace every aspect of myself and who I wanted to become, I opened my mind to more possibilities. I made decisions based on how I would like to feel. I have enjoyed getting comfortable with and developing my personal style. This has meant a change in hair, clothing and yes, even fragrance.

When you consider getting out of your comfort zone, do you picture doing something hard or perilous? How about reframing that to something fun, like a trip to the perfume counter? You see sometimes it is one small change that is instrumental in putting you into a new version of yourself. The perfume counter was that for me.

Not that long ago I would have felt intimidated. Then, one day I decided it was time. So, off I went and happily sought out the woman at the counter. She guided me to trying different scents and finding the one right for me. Every time I use it, it gives me a little lift and a reminder of how I am stepping into this new vision for myself. Setting goals, enlarging my idea of who I am and making decisions that will lead me to where I want to go. In effect, I have become an explorer of my own life.

This time of transition, of becoming an explorer, also means accepting the challenge to push against the resistance that sometimes pops up. As you change and grow, you will be pushing through old beliefs. That's when you get to decide which aspects of your personality you wish to embrace and which you want to adjust. It also means diligently letting go of regret. We all do the best we can at any given time in our lives, especially now as you create the next chapter of your life.

We can all benefit from the words of that wise woman Alice and indeed live by her example. Go ahead, set some goals, create the life you want and yes, stubbornly live.

## Life Transformation through the Power of Play

Transforming your life into one you are truly passionate about is an ongoing process, but it's not all about deep reflection and serious thoughts. Have you considered the place for play in your life?

If your life of late has been taken up with responsibility to others, paying bills and making big decisions, play can seem frivolous and pointless. But it is the very act of doing something for no reason other than you enjoy it, which is the point.

Letting go, allowing yourself to be in the moment, also known as mindfulness, allows your body to relax. To release some of the tension that your adult self takes on through the daily act of living.

Children use play as a means of learning about their world and themselves. It is also self-expression and connection. When is the last time you did something playful? Something in which you laughed and let yourself just be. If you are drawing a blank, as I did when I first tried to get back in touch with what brought me happiness, I simply chose to remember happier times. Consider the who, what and where of the memory.

When you were growing up, some play may have been done alone, but most of it was with other children such as siblings or friends. This means finding others willing to have some of those adventures with you. While we may not be able to be as spontaneous as children, it is possible to take on some of their spontaneous decision-making.

Consider these options: a trip to the beach and making a sandcastle; a bike ride and trying out a new set of bike paths; if you live in a snowy clime, building snowmen, going tobogganing or getting back on your skis.

You don't have to engage in activities with a cost to them; you can simply get out and make fun happen. Inviting play which has a physical element holds many opportunities for you to reacquaint yourself with your body. Play frees you from being concerned about the correct way of doing an activity and simply enjoy participating. Give yourself the pleasure of using whatever activities you choose to stretch yourself beyond what you might otherwise consider.

Combining an activity with others and making it more physical brings mental and physical benefits to you. The sedentary lifestyle which has evolved with technology is slowing down and, in some cases, eliminating simpler interactions with others, even isolating us if we aren't careful. The very act of group play not only increases the likelihood that devices are put down, but also increases much needed connection while creating new memories. All that and the potential to re-ignite a spark that may have dimmed over the years.

Play is the means of bringing others into our world.

After the solo portion of your journey to creating a life of meaning, bringing others into your world is a welcome addition. Using play from your younger self also frees you from the inclination to use alcohol to "relax you". As a child, you did not need anything to relax you to play the game, ride the bike or fly the kite. You just began and the relaxation and energy release followed.

Inviting play that has a physical element holds many opportunities for us to reacquaint ourselves with our bodies, to find the pleasure of using them outside the orchestrations of a gym and stretch ourselves beyond what we might otherwise consider.

Fun is also about letting go of worry and just doing. Truly being in the moment and letting loose. Play means that your goal is not about doing something perfectly. Rather, you are just doing it and accepting whatever occurs. Finally, it is also about the willingness not to take yourself too seriously and be able to laugh at yourself.

## Using "Remember When" as the Springboard towards Future Experiences

Just like play, past experiences are the means of rediscovering and re-introducing new options on how to create these next chapters of your life. "Remember when" serves as the beginning of what's next.

It is not about recreating the experience but rather recalling the elements that made it fun in the first place.

For instance, picture two twenty-something single women, bored on a Friday night. Neither are interested in the bar scene, and they are just itching for something different. For no clear reason other than it entered their minds and a car was available, and they could, they thought a road trip was the perfect idea.

Yes, that was me and a friend.

We decided an impromptu trip to see friends in another province was the best idea ever. We didn't pack, we had some cash and our credit cards. This was before cell phones, ATMs or roadside assistance. We gassed up the car and went—eight hours of music, talking and laughter. Miraculously our friends were home and good sports about us arriving on their doorstep. We still laugh about it.

Other than a great memory, how else do those types of stories serve you? When you are seeking ways to enrich and bring more joy into your everyday lives, it is likely to be the experiences which will lead the way and shed light on what is most important to you.

Stories are reminders of you who are at any given time. Beyond nostalgia, they can help you reconnect with those aspects of yourself that may have been put away as you embarked on other areas of your life.

## Your Experiences Are the Threads of Your Life

For my friend and me, the road trip isn't just a great story, it is also one about seizing the moment. Being okay with not knowing the outcome and of believing things would work out. Embracing the feeling we had nothing to lose in the doing of it.

The experience provides a framework for what is possible now, and what stands to be gained by acceptance of that attitude again.

While there are television shows I enjoy, it is unlikely I am going to recall and share them in one, five or twenty years down the road. The entertainment value may exist, but it is fleeting at best.

Experiences, however, are memorable because of what happened within them and they last long after the time in which they occurred. They are in fact, the threads of your life.

## Experiences as Springboards

Life stories are a series of experiences and needn't be expensive or involve travel or adventure. They can be found in the simplest scenarios and involve just one thing, something worth retelling. It could be something you learned, something that surprised you about yourself or someone else. They can have deep meaning or be life-changing or they can inspire wonder, peace or awe. Experiences can set your imagination on fire or spark your curiosity. They can connect you with others who share them or be a defining moment that helps you make a decision.

If you are in the process of creating a new chapter, and there are so many in our lives, experiences that have helped you on your path are worth exploring. They can also be great springboards for creating more of what you want.

Life is what we make it and experiences are the road to creating the who, what and how in our lives.

## Understanding the Power of Your Thoughts

Leading spiritual teachers have long understood the power of our thoughts and what they bring into our lives. No doubt you've heard the idea that where we place our attention is what comes to us.

In 2010 when the empty nest loomed, I realized I was going to have more time available to me than I had for a long time. The question became: How did I want to spend the time and with whom?

Accepting that my husband was disinterested in many of the things that brought me enjoyment meant taking responsibility to be the creator of the experiences I wanted. My friendship circle had dwindled and increasing the number of friends became a part of my quest.

I decided to try volunteering at a local music festival as the means of accomplishing one part of my life creating mission. Instead of going by myself I chose to find a way to contribute; volunteering allowed me to do that.

Little could I imagine that choosing the path of volunteering would lead me into a new circle of friends and open the door to other areas of interest.

The summer music event occurs over four days at the start of summer. I signed up to volunteer for three of the four days. Each day I reported to the volunteer tent, awaiting my assignment. Each day they took me to one spot, only to shift me to the one I'd been the day before. Each time, the same volunteer was there and each time, we engaged in ever widening circles of conversation.

The volunteer shifts were several hours long, and we had time to get to know each other. At the close of my third day, I realized that if I wanted to see this woman again, it was up to me to create the opportunity.

I took a chance, asking her if she would be interested in getting together for coffee sometime after the event. Much to my delight, she was open to this and thus began a new and much needed friendship. It also meant that through her I was welcomed into a larger group, a spiritual book club. Something else I had set as my intention—the desire to meet others on the path of spiritual and personal growth.

When you express your wants, you might be surprised to find how the universe has your back. First might come the idea of how to begin accessing the experiences you seek, then following through and seeing where the tide takes you. It is about simultaneously asking and receiving and then once again, defining that which you want.

If you are interested in knowing more about how to attract what you want, I suggest you read the book by Esther and Jerry Hicks, Ask and It Is Given.

This was the beginning of my lessons in the power of asking for what I want and then opening to the opportunities to allow it to occur. I didn't know how it would happen but knew only that I was ready. This has proven itself to me time and again, from finding friends to meeting people with the skills and knowledge to grow my life personally and professionally.

My readiness for finding more of the things I love led me to the idea of volunteering at an event. This method, volunteering, increased my chances of meeting other people who similarly enjoyed that interest. That's just logic, right? Sure. But that continued chance meeting of a woman who was interesting, well read and had similar interests, that was the universe giving me what I said I wanted.

I wasn't looking for a friend to go and get my nails done with. I was searching for someone who was capable and interested in having deeper conversations. I stated my intention and the universe provided. If it were to become more than that, it was up to me. Two sayings combined into one: Let go and let god and god helps those who help themselves.

Whether we call it universe, source or god, I believe that there is a greater power at work. One which is responsive to what we say we want. Opportunities will arise, but it's up to us to accept them and act on their potential.

## The Pillars of Change—Curiosity, Comfort Zones and Synchronicity

One of the difficulties as you begin the work of defining what you want, is defining what those wants are. We can become so accustomed to meeting the needs and wants of others, that we completely lose track of ourselves. This is where curiosity can become your new, life-changing friend.

Have you ever watched a young child when they are out in the natural world? Everything is new and everything is yet to be discovered. Young children don't get bored because they are curious and for them, everything is a new adventure.

Curiosity is what greases the inner world towards discovery of yourself and of how and what you have to contribute to the world. If you have ever thought or said the following, your curiosity might need a tune up: "There has been no good music since ________." "I don't go to those festivals/events/plays because I don't have anything in common with those people."

"Don't," "won't" and "never" all have one thing in common. They are prime ways to kill curiosity and an excellent way to create a narrow and lackluster life.

## Trying New Things Opens You Up

Trying new things, going to new places (even in your own city) is the gateway to finding new gems and new forms of pleasure. Creating new first times can be exhilarating. They can also provide the fodder for new conversations and new ideas. Trying new things is not a commitment to doing that thing again; instead, it is simply a matter of opening to the world around you.

Curiosity is about seeing, doing and asking questions. To foster curiosity, the easiest place to start is to find an existing event that sparks your interest. Something just a little outside your known world which allows you to observe or participate at whatever level you are comfortable.

In my area of the world, there is an event that occurs every time the calendar aligns a Friday on the 13th. The small town of Port Dover in southwestern Ontario becomes a motorcycling destination. Thousands descend with or without motorcycles, for a day of machines, their leather-clad riders and the people wishing to witness the spectacle. I don't own a motorcycle, nor do I own any leather clothing, however having never attended this "event", I think it could be a great people-watching activity. Possibly an opportunity to learn new things and meet new people.

The experience is also one rich with potential for reflection.

When you insert yourself into a new experience or environment, you may have unexpected feelings such as excitement, anxiety, curiosity or boredom. Each of these feelings can lead to greater insights about your emotional state and even your openness for discovery. Taking the time to do a check-in of your emotions can help you determine whether there are greater opportunities for self-discovery.

For instance, when you do that emotional check-in at an event such as the motorcycle gathering, you may notice how comfortable or not you are within this different experience. If you are uncomfortable, how were you uncomfortable? Or, did you find yourself in conversation with anybody, either casually or at greater depth?

If you are uncomfortable, this is an invitation to look more closely at your discomfort. Is it because the people or the atmosphere challenges your way of thinking? Or perhaps you feel challenged by what you think you are capable of or of what interests you? Does it rub up against who you think you are and who you might be, if you were to participate in the event or place?

Have some fun. Imagine yourself in the clothing or with a motorcycle? How does that feel?

Reflection is the place where growth resides. Change occurs slowly and one of the best ways of fostering it is to push the boundaries of what you are comfortable with. This is a life-long effort taken in small steps, so that you can continue your forward movement. Pushing your comfort zone means accepting that you are likely to experience the sweaty palms and nerves of putting yourself, even marginally, into something new.

Pushing your comfort zone is a bit daunting at first, especially if you are out of practice. What is surprising though, is that while pushing through your discomfort always takes effort, every time you do, you feel better. Happier even.

“Do one thing each day that scares you.” Eleanor Roosevelt

My life in the last five years has been a lot of movement out of the known zone to the unknown. Each time requires a bit of a personal pep talk, a reminder that past efforts have been successful. The pep talk and reminders become a part of the resilience toolbox. The means of moving forward, rebounding or transforming old unhelpful thoughts to new and more powerful ones.

Why bother with these efforts?

Because complacency can kick in and then maybe "good enough" and then even "settle for".

Those attitudes don't serve you well. Don't get me wrong, it's a great thing to be appreciative of what you have and of enjoying the moment. Very good in fact, but like so many other things, appreciation and enjoyment can become dulled by the same old, same old routine we set ourselves up for. Current research tells us that continuing to challenge ourselves, physically and intellectually helps prevent Alzheimer's and dementia. It also does wonders for our overall happiness. While you might not be ready to do one new thing each day that scares you, you may want to consider incremental challenges.

## New Experiences Create New Stories

The intriguing part of breaking out of your comfort zone is that you discover beliefs and stories of yourself you were unaware of. It's a journey of self-discovery.

We all seem to have stories of ourselves that we acquire over time and which can become unyielding and unbending. Coats of armor that soon begin to block out the potential for new interactions and possibilities. Old stories can weigh us down, and before long, we can't tell the difference between a foundation and protective gear.

## Retiring Old Stories and Creating New

At the age of 69, Donna McCracken was sure she was no artist. However, when an acquaintance invited her to a painting class, she gamely accepted. There she found a skilled instructor, encouraging classmates, and a chance to build new skills. Six years later, McCracken's home overflows with her work and is bought by those who appreciate her talents. She's found a passion she did not realize existed, simply by saying yes. She's also changed her beliefs about her artistic talents and yes, her story.

How many old stories continue to be a part of your inner dialogue? Have you ever found yourself uttering statements like, "I don't do that" or "I'm no good at that"? Chances are good you are guilty of cheating yourself out of a bigger life.

Christie Murray is a successful entrepreneur who runs a busy, in-demand hair salon from her home.

Her bubbly, infectious laugh, and genuine interest in her clients results in frequent invitations to activities and events. Eight years ago, one such invitation came via a "girl's night out" group activity—a pole dancing class. Despite some hesitation, she nevertheless accepted and what she found went far beyond her preconceived notions. Physically demanding as well as artistic, it is now a part of her everyday life.

Since the first class, she's not only taken more classes but has gone on to teach them. She attends competitions and her interest in becoming more skilled has pushed her to take her first solo plane trip out of country to train with professional coaches.

There's no doubt when talking to her, that she's discovered an interest that has challenged and changed her ideas about her own physical and mental capabilities.

Upon the end of Valerie Edward's marriage in her 30s, she felt a need to challenge herself, and break out of her shell. She accepted an invitation to rock climb. To her surprise, she found the physical challenge, coupled with the solo skills much more to her preference. She no longer considers herself non-athletic. Rather, her identity now includes the story of her physical strength and preference of outdoor sports instead of school team sports.

No one comes to these activities with a story of pre-existing skill. Each of these people accept and live the credo, "nothing ventured nothing gained." They are exhibiting the growth mindset as defined by Dweck. Instead of worrying about their level of competency and whether they may or may not be "naturals", they embrace the challenge of trying something new. They are willing to be beginners and put in the effort to become better, believing that the possibility to improve is realistic.

If your comfort zone hasn't been stretched for a while, you don't need to be taking life-altering steps to challenge yourself. That's a sure way to retreat into the rabbit hole and not re-emerge for a good long time.

Developing a sense of wonder, of being open to the world and noticing what you previously walked by, all foster curiosity and in turn that nurtures your soul.

A sense of curiosity will most certainly open the pathways towards your discovery of what you truly want. Its dual role of narrowing and expanding your interests, creates a place to challenge your comfort zone, helping you define your inner desires.

And from there, synchronicity has a place to land and invite you further into unimagined possibility.

# Chapter 9: On the Path of Change

**"The journey between who you once were and who you are becoming is where the dance of life really takes place."**
**Barbara De Angelis**

Congratulations, you are on the path to change! Are you ready for all the great things to come your way? At this point, it's beneficial to consider the power of pace.

You've begun to invite new experiences and new people into your life. You're immersed in new information, opportunities, and ways of living. It's exhilarating, but possibly just a little overwhelming too.

When life begins to widen, it's easy not to see the impact of suddenly having many choices and opportunities from which to choose. It can be a potential pitfall.

The first part of the journey is a rediscovery of yourself. The second is how to fit it all together without becoming overwhelmed and shutting down.

As counterintuitive as it may seem, this is where you are going to begin learning how to say no.

Even when there are a lot of great choices, choosing the what, when and why enhances your overall plans for the directions you want to take. Saying no doesn't mean never, it can simply be not now.

If you've been a people pleaser, this is a hard lesson. It means, once again, deciding what is most important for you and your goals. It's about understanding that saying no to one thing is saying yes to something else.

Here's what I've learned about saying no:

1. I have the time to pursue the goals I've set out for myself. Whether that's writing more, making sales calls, or creating new connections. Saying no means staying true to what I've established as important.
2. Saying no is a form of self-care. It means that I'm not trying to fit more into an already busy day and adding stress or worry to my schedule. Looking after myself means setting some boundaries: No is a boundary.
3. No means that I take myself seriously, that I respect myself.
4. No means I love myself and those people and projects I already have in my life enough to continue to invest my energy in them. I won't

let that get stretched and thinned out by trying to be more or do more than what makes my life happy and healthy.

5. No is a signal that I stand strong in my decisions.

The more you understand yourself and your needs, the easier it becomes to make those choices.

## Self-care during Times of Transition

As you get closer to living the life you wish, there will be some hills and valleys as you define in more detail what you need to remain healthy. You are undergoing an intense period of change in which it's quite possible many areas of your life are changing at the same time.

Are you able to step back and be mindful to your needs?

In times of change, it's important to tend your mental health and add to your resiliency toolbox. One area that's often overlooked is time in nature. Regardless of how much we may enjoy urban trappings, experiences within nature hold healing properties.

The value of spending time in nature is gaining momentum as scientists, healthcare practitioners, educators, and the public discover its physical and mental benefits.

Play time in nature (or green space) increases the capacity and development of creativity, problem-solving, and intellect in children (Kellert, 2005). I rather wonder if it doesn't still support those cognitive functions within adults.

Plugging into nature and sharing the experience with others creates new stories and memories that last over the years. It creates a sense of connection and being part of something bigger than ourselves. Depending on the setting, it can also inspire awe. According to researchers, that has a positive impact too.

My feelings of contentment and well-being are consistent with studies done by environmental psychologists. In fact, more and more healthcare centers are designing natural spaces for the use and view of their patients. Studies show that patients who have a view of the natural world go home sooner than those with views of walls.

Regardless of your age, profession, or relationship status, you owe it to yourself to re-engage with the natural world. The sights, sounds, and smells of nature soothe us as few things can. Consider taking some time to explore your options, and then schedule it in. I think you'll find that it adds a depth and sense of enjoyment to your life that may have gone missing.

## Taking Time to Smell the Roses

With everything that is going on in your changing world, are you able to slow down and reflect? Cultivating practices of meditation, reflection, appreciation, and gratitude will help you stay grounded as you navigate the many internal and external changes.

I first began to meditate when I was receiving trauma counselling. The psychologist suggested it as a daily self-care measure. I continue to find it as helpful now as I did then. As I was learning how to meditate, I initially used guided meditations and joined in with some of Deepak Chopra's online meditation offerings. Over time though, I found others to do on my own.

Meditation has been gaining acceptance in the Western world over the last decade, once modern science had the means to prove its effectiveness. The use of MRIs showing brain activity allowed scientists to view which areas of the brain lit up and which calmed down. Meditation has gone from anecdotal reports to data-supported evidence.

So much of our Western culture is about productivity and constant motion. Recovering the ability to slow down and rest, both mentally and physically, is slowly gaining traction.

My meditation occurs during the final portion of my daily walk. A trail winds through an old, overgrown soccer field. It's my little hit of nature in the middle of an urban setting. Every morning, this trail is the backdrop to my morning meditation.

Once I step foot on the trail, I physically stop and bring myself into the present. I embrace the now, aware of the sunlight and the dew, the wildflowers and the birds. I take in a breath and in my mind the very first meditation/affirmation is: I am the creator of all my experiences.

I find this to be both powerful and calming. Along with the other statements regarding abundance and doing work I love; it sets me up for a happy day.

Working alone, especially at the beginning of this new venture, I'm sometimes prone to discouragement. Like any new business, there is currently more money going out than coming in. That can leave me feeling a little anxious and down.

Nevertheless, the setting and the meditation restore my set point. I'm in control of my feelings, my thoughts, and my actions.

Is meditation right for you? I personally think everyone can benefit from its use. We are a go, go, go society, but a consistent practice of building in some slow thinking can build mental health. Happily, it can be done at no cost and with no special tools.

## The Power of Gratitude

Similar to meditation, an attitude of gratitude can be transformative.

In our everyday life, it's easy to become more aware of the problems and small daily inconveniences than the things that are going right. Consistently focusing on all that you appreciate shifts your attention and the energy that you are putting into the world.

Gratitude and appreciation help re-focus and bring more of the good into your line of sight. Noticing, even at the smallest level, can be a way to bring you back to a lighter spirit.

If you decide to make nature a more regular part of your life, then it can be an easy way to begin your appreciation. For instance, I take a moment to notice the deep blue of the morning glory flowers cascading over the fence. Or I might note my appreciation and gratitude of the small patio at which I often write. I'll jot down the little visits of wildlife that make me smile, like the chipmunk I've come to recognize due to his short tail, as he races from one fence to another.

Then, I'll take a moment to appreciate the people who are supportive of me and all my new endeavours. I am grateful for it all.

You may start with a negative demeanor but before long find yourself immersed in appreciation for what and where your life is taking you. By bringing appreciation and gratitude into your day, you add to both the spirit and tone of your daily life.

## How Art Imitates Life

While on the road to change, sometimes you need reminders about how and why your actions are important. While you're on a personal journey of transformation, it's worth knowing that your actions impact others. Without intending it, you're a role model to others and what is possible in their lives.

I came to understand this as I reflected on who I found inspiring. Of course, I could name people on the world stage, but they feel remote from us, don't they? So, who then might fall under the title inspirer?

Inspiration, admiration, and motivation can find us just about anywhere. Even at a local music hall during an open mic night.

Over the course of the evening, musicians of all ages sat or stood on a small stage. They came to play and sing their original music or that of others. In a small room on a small stage, each performer embraced the vulnerability of being seen. They found courage and accepted full responsibility for whatever they produced in the time they were there.

All ages, mostly men, came to the stage differently and approached their music differently. Some confidently set up and began while others were more tentative. Some gave their work an introduction and explanation, and others spent time tuning their instruments.

One older gentleman, accompanied by his sister and a friend, fairly quivered before beginning. As I watched, it occurred to me the truth that art mimics life. None were performing because they expected stardom or discovery. They performed because the music was in them and they needed to express it.

## What Version of Your Life Awaits Expression?

A similar example occurs between our interpretation of ideas and experiences. We share the human experience regardless of cultures and countries. Yet each of us comes to it with a different understanding. We pull something different from it. Just like music.

An original song could be performed by ten different artists. Fifty-plus years after Simon & Garfunkel recorded "Sounds of Silence," there was a new interpretation by Disturbed, an artist you wouldn't expect to cover it. His version was backed by classical artists and sung with strength and depth. It resonated with many listeners, including some who may never have heard the original version.

He brought to life, in his own unique way, the sentiments expressed in the song. He proved it to be relevant and still needing to be heard.

## Full Expression of Our Whole Self

It could be said, by those with a narrower frame of mind, that such depth of emotion is unexpected from "that kind of artist." Check out his YouTube channel. You'll see an entirely different person than you might expect from hearing his recording of the Simon & Garfunkel classic.

This is a great example of how none of us are just one thing. We fail ourselves and others when we believe that only this person or that person has full access to expressing life in all its varied forms. Believing that, we stand to lose richer ways of understanding and creating the lives we want.

## Self-imposed Boundaries

We set up self-imposed boundaries that keep our lives and worlds small. Why? Because we don't believe we're able to move beyond what we think we already know, or who we believe ourselves to be.

Then we meet someone, an everyday person whose life has challenged them to push beyond those boundaries. Someone like*Faith Stone.

I met *Faith while working for a non-profit organization. She'd seen our posting for volunteers for our summer camp. A bubbly, happy, warm person, she immediately had me wanting to get to know her better. As we chatted, I learned that she came from a family dedicated to hard work and achievement and that she was in university taking courses in the arts and business. Midway through her schooling she was in a motor vehicle accident and suffered a major brain injury.

This information explained why she got a ride out to our facility. She wasn't yet cleared to drive again.

When she came to talk with me about her desire to volunteer, she was upfront about her situation. She said she wasn't sure if she could do a whole day, but really wanted to give it a try. She had her doctor's clearance to volunteer, but she'd have some appointments with her neurosurgeon necessitating a few missed days.

At no time did she say "I can't." It was always "I can." She focused on possibilities, not obstacles. She came to offer what she'd like to do, if we were willing. That was inspiring.

We brought her on as a volunteer, and she soon became a favorite among staff for her can do attitude. She exemplified initiative and enjoyment of her position. Despite her challenges with fatigue and at times excruciating headaches, she'd always arrive ready to work.

Since then, and despite the physical challenges, she persevered and graduated on time. She credits the support and understanding from her professors and family, but I have no doubt that in addition to that, it was her sheer desire and commitment to completing the goal that saw her through. It was never if she would finish but how.

I don't know if there's an answer as to why some people take that positive attitude. I do believe, however, that we can all foster it. Life is going to present us with mountains, and only we can decide whether we'll climb them.

Sometimes, to stay the course, we just need to watch others who are also finding their way in living lives of intention and purpose. Faith Stone is one of many who reminds me of the reasons to do so.

If you want to live an inspired life, attack life with energy and gusto. Put away the "I can't" thinking and replace it with "I can." You will need help; we all do. That's not a source of weakness.

Whether you realize it or not, your decision to become fully you impacts the lives of those around you.

None of us knows how we touch the lives of others until we set ourselves free. It requires being seen as we are. Others need your voice and your interpretation. They need your perspective. You can achieve this by showing up and choosing to fully live.

# Chapter 10: Stay the Course

**"All changes ... have their melancholy; for what we leave behind us is a part of ourselves; we must die to one life before we can enter another."**

**Anatole France**

When I left my home province, I said goodbyes, many of them. At the time, I neither realized exactly how big a move it was nor the internal shifts to come.

Now I'm witness to the same psychological shift my son and his partner are making in a continental move. From one country, across an honest-to-goodness ocean, to another.

They've begun the process of goodbyes.

Goodbye not just to people, but to places and activities they've enjoyed. Goodbye to the laid-back culture of west coast Canada, with arguably some of the most beautiful scenery in the world.

The time has come for them, however, to move on, explore, and expand their worlds.

## Exterior Change Is the Least of It

Goodbye is the recognition that the person you were when you arrived isn't the person who's leaving.

If it were, you wouldn't be making this move.

When we look at life with a forward intent, there will always be some part of ourselves we must release. The outward journey, from one geographical location to another, is small in comparison to what is taking place within.

When I left my home province, I was a twenty-five-year-old university graduate who thought she had met and was marrying a man with whom she would spend the rest of her years. The move away helped me create a distance from the family I loved, but who were largely toxic to me. I didn't really come to know that until later.

When you decide that you are ready to embrace something new, when your mind aches for it, and you follow that yearning, you are also accepting change.

## Saying Goodbye: The Pain and Promise of Change

The biggest changes, those deaths of identity, are both painful and exhilarating. They require letting go of ideological and societal ideas of success so that the growth of a new identity can emerge.

While it may be a cliché to think of the caterpillar's metamorphosis to butterfly, it has its place.

Accepting the forward movement, listening and acting upon our internal drive to be more than how we started, results in an equally dramatic change.

The person I was three decades ago bears little resemblance to the person who writes today.

I may have wished to be writing then, but I felt I had little of value to say that would be helpful to others. I certainly couldn't conceive of breaking away from tradition—be it from the church into which I had been indoctrinated or from the marital promise of 'til death we do part.

None of my changes were easy. Each felt as if I was ripping off a layer of skin. Yet, even the expectation and experience of pain hurt less than making no changes at all. Difficult decisions, but nevertheless, the right ones.

## Growth Shifts and Transforms the Views

As I watch my son and his partner prepare for the great unknown, I applaud their joint and singular transformations. The duo to whom I say goodbye will not be the duo to whom I say hello in four years.

Their ideas of themselves, the world, and themselves in the world, will have shifted.

Of course, that's true for me too. Who I am now will surely have changed, becoming a thread in the larger tapestry of my life.

## Evolving Goals

How do we maintain the forward motion? Novelty, and you don't have to move countries to achieve it.

Novelty, the willingness to try new things, is good for body and mind. While we might say we are perfectly happy sticking to our well versed and predictable patterns of behaviour, science tells us to re-think that.

We now know that besides challenging our brain by doing activities like puzzles or learning a new language, it's beneficial to move our bodies. It helps to ward off Alzheimer's and dementia. By combining novelty and movement, we are doubling up on the benefits of both.

There's also the fun factor. Yeah, fun.

Why do you think people choose to go on rollercoasters, travel, or try a new restaurant? Because despite the grumblings about not liking change, we crave it. A little dash of the unknown, a little spice of excitement, gets our proverbial juices flowing.

## Novelty under a Moonlit Sky

A few weekends ago I headed out for a moonlight bike ride. My partner and I joined a dozen or so other intrepid cyclists and hit the city streets under a full moon. It got really interesting when we went off the well-lit streets and onto the unlit bike paths. Especially since they were all foreign to me.

There were a couple of times I might have uttered a quiet "shit" when rounding one turn only to find another. We were going at a pretty good clip. My headlight was on, but I quickly concluded that a stronger light was needed. Nevertheless, we did the trip, following the cyclists ahead of us and from time to time, stopping for a drink of water and a view of the city.

We went about twenty-five kilometers, when all was said and done. Needless to say, I slept well. I'm also happy to report that my body took kindly to the exercise, which is encouraging. It means more forays are possible.

A night bike ride might not be the most exciting thing you have done, nor does it need to be. That's not the objective. What I'm encouraging is that you consider some new possibilities in your life.

## You Have to Be Fully Present

Doing something that stretches you out of the everyday routine is key to putting a spring in your step and having a new conversational tidbit to share. It should be something that requires all your attention and allows you to open fully, instead of hanging back at the edges.

This is as true at work as it is in our personal lives.

Look around your workplace, talk to your colleagues, and see what projects they have going on. Investigate where you might be able to try your hand at something new, just for the fun of it.

When we start asking questions, seek the unknown and novel; it's surprising what's hidden in plain sight.

You don't have to travel abroad. As it turns out, there are surprising opportunities right where you live. You need only seek them out. A quick look in the paper shows listings for a pop-up music jam, fall fairs, and historical tours. It's not what you do, but that you do it.

Then, there are the internal dreams, awaiting expression.

## To Dream, Perchance to Live

I would modify Shakespeare's quote to say "to dream, perchance to live." By following my dreams, I continue to become more completely myself. I am discovering parts of myself I didn't know existed. It's exhilarating and a little frightening all at the same time. If there's a dual gift I could bestow, it's curiosity and the willingness to follow your dreams. Both make life a pretty fantastic journey.

Transitions from one point to the next will continue, if you keep engaging with the world. It's within the process of transition that wise choices must be made. From time to time, do less. It will free you up to do more.

It might be occasionally uncomfortable but growing into your next adventure and challenge creates a richness and depth you can barely imagine.

## Practice Resilience

There's no doubt that life is going to continue to deliver challenges. This is why it's so important to continue to build resilience.

I've come to think of resiliency as an emotional core. Just like our physical core, it needs regular attention. If you've ever tried to get back into your fitness regimen after a holiday or being sick, you know that your body is not the way you left it. It will take time to get it back to where you were.

The same is true of our emotional core.

Resiliency is our ability to overcome life's hurdles. Some definitions include adversity, but I choose to expand that to hurdles, the experiences that knock us off our game. Even positive experiences—such as moving or having a baby—need a workout of our emotional core. New surroundings, new demands, and new roles are all stressful and require a tool kit of sorts to work through.

Here's what I know. When we are faced with difficult situations and transition, we need people around.

When life hands you lemons...connect with your friends, in person if possible. You see there are some situations that just require people near you. Technology does a lot, but it can't match what happens when you are physically with someone.

I've learned this through personal experiences and volunteering as part of a victim services organization. Sometimes there really aren't words for what's going on. That's where a hug, or the ability to sit quietly and be a presence is needed. For the many ways that technology allows us to keep in touch, to communicate, it will never be able to replicate being beside someone.

How well are you keeping up your friendships and relationships? Are you connecting through more than a text or social media? They do in a pinch or when geography doesn't make it possible for an in-person interaction. However, for too many of us, it's become our go-to means of connecting.

In the past, when we lived in smaller and more traditional communities, in-person interactions happened all the time. Now, we must try to see others in a regular and healthy manner.

One that helped me as I found my way through mid-life singlehood was being invited into a weekly Sunday dinner event. Created by friends, as a means of connecting with each other, like the old family meals we may have grown up with. That inclusiveness ensured I broke the weekend isolation I would have otherwise experienced.

Belonging is a fundamental need. Continuing to fuel belonging and reaching out is necessary. It's the foundation of how we then navigate the harder sections of our lives.

Belonging, creating the pathways to connection which last over time, is an important part of our resilience. It doesn't just happen; belonging requires effort, forethought and consistency.

Real relationships are also based on reciprocity.

Recently, when my daughter received news that her best friend's father had passed away, she reached out. Not just at the moment, nor in the short-term or even just to her friend. She has stopped in to visit both her friend and her friend's now-widowed mother, even weeks after the funeral, because she has learned how important this is.

It's common for people to fall away after the death of someone, or when there is a chronic illness. I fear that timeline has shortened even more with the advent of technology. We're learning to scroll through, hit "like" or create a short message and move on. What's happening less and less is stopping in to see or talk to the person on an individual basis.

When I received bad news about a family friend, I felt a strong desire to connect. With the person, but also with others with whom I share the connection. It's almost as if we too need the solidity and comfort of someone else feeling the depth of pain. We seek understanding and we seek others who belong to this group.

We see this in the larger context too. Tragedies, be they deliberate or accidental, bring people together. We seek solace with others.

## Your Emotional Core

We are all connected in a spider web of relationships that span family, work, school, hobbies, and our online and offline communities. Each of these offer different experiences and feelings. They also give us varying levels of satisfaction and safety within our worlds. From the perspective of resilience, this is a good thing. In fact, managing our lives and the problems that arise all depend on our array of connections.

Are all your relationships intact? How good are you at tending them? Are there a few people who have slipped off your radar? It happens, right? Life is busy. Days and then weeks and even months can slide by and you haven't connected.

Now's the time my friends. Consider it preventative maintenance and...it's fun!

Whatever reason brought you together, the connection and enjoyment you feel when you're with them is undoubtedly still there. It may take some doing, but the payoff is excellent.

## Change Your Routine

Doing the same old thing with the same old people is easy, but it isn't in our best interest. Even taking the same route to work or school every day can be a barrier to experience. Auto pilot kicks in as you repeat your activities, and your world narrows. When you start interacting with others on the fringes of your circle, friends of friends perhaps, or acquaintances, it fires up different parts of your personality. They may be people with whom you struck up an initial friendship but have allowed to slide to the sides of your life.

Think of the friend with whom you share a love of witty greeting cards or the one that's always reading some interesting article or book. What about the person who has the "willing to try anything" flair? You know, just enough dare and spontaneity that you find yourself willing to try a new ride at the fair or sign up for a class you wouldn't consider doing on your own.

Those connections are so important. They help keep us anchored in our lives and to ourselves. And then, yes, when life hands you an obstacle, you've tended your relationships, so you're not left trying to manage all on your own.

And, might I add, it's best to widen your network of friends  if you find it has shrunk due to events such as moves or job changes.

## Expand Your Connections

It's also a good idea to take an "inventory" of where your friends and close relationships are from. If you see that some areas are more heavily weighted than others—such as work or family—it's worth considering the impact should you change jobs or retire. And, if you and your family are all coping with the same situation, it's helpful to have others to whom you can turn.

There's no right or magic number to your connection network. Your network's biggest asset is its proximity to you. While technology is great, friends from afar can't provide you with needed in-person support. As society changes and more people are living on their own, with fewer interactions with others, I'd like to suggest we all re-think our daily lives. Throw the net wider, invite more people in and then ensure you are tending to each other.

## Creating, Caring for, and Maintaining Happiness

Happiness on a budget is something we don't discuss enough. If we believe what we see on social media, everyone is out there enjoying fabulous vacations, trips, and experiences. We see less of low-key, low-cost, but equally enjoyable pursuits. That's a shame, because the reality is that most of us don't have the means to support high-end all the time.

Those who are saving for a big purchase, have a new baby, are supporting kids in post-secondary education, or living modestly on retirement funds, may not be able to embark on any of those kinds of adventures.

Just like money can't buy you love, it also doesn't have to be the only variable in happiness. Treat this stage as an adventure in living life to the fullest and accept the challenge of doing so in a "fiscally responsible manner." No-cost, low-cost or surplus gifting or exchanges are great ways to enjoy yourself.

## Happiness Is Child's Play

Revisiting some childhood pleasures is one way to connect with the fun inside that is just waiting to be released. My foray into play has brought me back to bike riding, Frisbee, backgammon, and croquet. Guess what? They are all free.

Each game has given me back carefree, in-the-moment, childlike laughter. And that's a good thing. Letting go and being in the moment (also known as mindfulness) allows the body to relax. It releases some of the tension that our adult selves take on through the daily act of living.

I am fortunate to live in an area with a lot of "by donation" festivals, offering me not just musical interests, but also people-watching. This completely free and ever-so-interesting opportunity to people-watch gives me glimpses into a bigger world. It places me among parents with young children, couples of all ages, groups of friends, people on their own, and people of varied backgrounds and cultures. From clothing to hairstyles to their interactions with each other, all are rich moments in the kaleidoscope of the event.

## Sharing, Gifting, Exchanging

Surplus gifting or exchanges can include offering a good friend the use of your home while you are away. I have friends who live in the country and from time to time, I house-sit and enjoy their property. They get peace of mind, and I get peace of place. Win, win.

Sometimes we receive or have available to us tickets for special events like concerts, theatre, or sports games. This is often true for corporations with box seats, who, from time to time, offer employees tickets at reduced price or no-cost. Consider asking a friend you haven't seen for a while to attend with you. It's an excellent way to re-establish your friendship and create a new memory for you both.

Keeping in touch with and nourishing your friendships is an important part of growing your personal resilience and happiness quotient. Shared activities and experiences are cornerstones of memory building, which is a foundation of the history you share with someone.

Then, there's the old-fashioned getting together over a home-cooked meal. My sanity as a young mother was preserved by an informal weekly playgroup. Potluck style and a chance to be with other mothers and some fathers to enjoy not just good food, but great company. Whether or not you have children, and regardless of your age, this is a valid option for a weekly "Sunday lunch or dinner." Enjoying good food together, sharing conversation, and creating a new tradition are budget-friendly and definitely raise the happiness meter.

## Is Your Next Great Passion Just a Bulletin Board Away?

Have you been to your local library lately? So many of us are accustomed to buying online that we forget there are great resources on our doorsteps. Libraries also happen to contain those good old-fashioned bulletin boards. You know, the ones in which local groups, emerging artists, and others with something to offer put up a flyer. Who knows, your next great passion might be awaiting discovery among the notices tacked up for dog walking and fundraisers.

There's a lot to be enjoyed in your own backyard and community. The more you invest yourself in the place where you live, the more likely you will find satisfaction and enjoyment right where you are. That kind of happiness is a treasure, and it's available to you no matter what your budget might be.

## Maintaining Happiness by Creating Technology Boundaries

Science tells us that we are not as good at multi-tasking as we think, and the constant interruptions take us away from a focused approach to the task at hand. The interruption requires a longer time for our brains to re-engage with the task and to make progress again.

What does this have to do with happiness?

It comes back to making decisions about when you are available, to whom, and under what circumstances. It's about understanding that taking down time is important to recharge and be ready for the next "to-do" on your list. If you are never free from technology, if there's a part of your brain always ready to receive and respond to something outside of your present circumstance, then you are in a constant state of tension. Consistent tension, even in small amounts, wears a person down.

## Happiness in the Moment

Being fully in the moment is a gift to your whole self. It facilitates an ability to take in the beauty of a winter scene, enjoy the antics of squirrels racing after each other, or be fully attentive when a person you care about is talking to you.

Technology is here to stay, and it has brought us many benefits. How we use it and its many applications is the challenge of setting our expectations of it and of ourselves. Will we allow it to add to or decrease our happiness? Are we using it to project ourselves as we are or absorbing an image of who we think we need to be? It's quite acceptable, perhaps even radical, to consider taking technology breaks. Announce that you are going to be offline. Then, put the phone, tablet, or laptop away and just be.

The true power of self-leadership is understanding that by exercising choice, by making decisions to move forward, we activate greater motivation within ourselves. Satisfaction and enjoyment ensue.

# Conclusion:

We will all face obstacles in our lives and it is self-leadership that will help us to transform them into opportunities to create lives of meaning and purpose. Life is what we make it regardless of the inevitable hurdles, disappointments and sorrows. For some of us, the journey is a little rockier, but no matter what your age or stage of life, there remain plenty of choices about how to approach and resolve them. You needn't settle for what has been or what others expect of you.

Choosing to create a life in which you are fully present, to others and to yourself, doesn't happen overnight and it doesn't happen without support. By freeing yourself to connect with others as you make your journey, you will also experience moments of laughter, gratitude and joy.

You don't have to wait for your subconscious to send you messages through your dreams, as I did. That dream, of being a passenger without control was upsetting but it also served as the spark for me to examine my life and accept responsibility.

Once I had the courage to look and begin to make the necessary changes, the subconscious responded in kind.

Two years later, having survived the messy middle of transition, a brief dream replaced the nightmare, containing a very different message.

This time, as I approached a shiny new car, a man at my side, I confidently looked him square in the face and said, "I'll drive."

You owe it to yourself to fully express the gift of life that you have. Each of us is so much more than the roles and stages of life through which we pass. Are you ready to embrace possibility and choose your way?

This has been my Journey to Joy and I hope that by sharing my experiences and all I have learned so far, that it will give you a measure of courage or hope to seek out your own path. By choosing to live your life on your terms, in line with your values and vision, I have every confidence that you will craft your own unique path to creating a life of deep meaning and joy.

# Appendix 1

## Wheel of Life

Instructions: Consider each category in turn, and on a scale of 0 (low) which is closest to the centre and 10 the furthest out, place an x where you feel your life is right now. Don't over think this!

Now, join up the x marks – does your life look balanced or in line with what you want? Are there areas where you could pull back a little in order to have more time and energy to spend on others?

Balance isn't about having 10s in every area, as time and energy and even resources fluctuate, but you now have a graphic representation of where you are and where you may want to focus.

The challenge now is to transform this knowledge and desire for a more balanced life into a positive program of action.

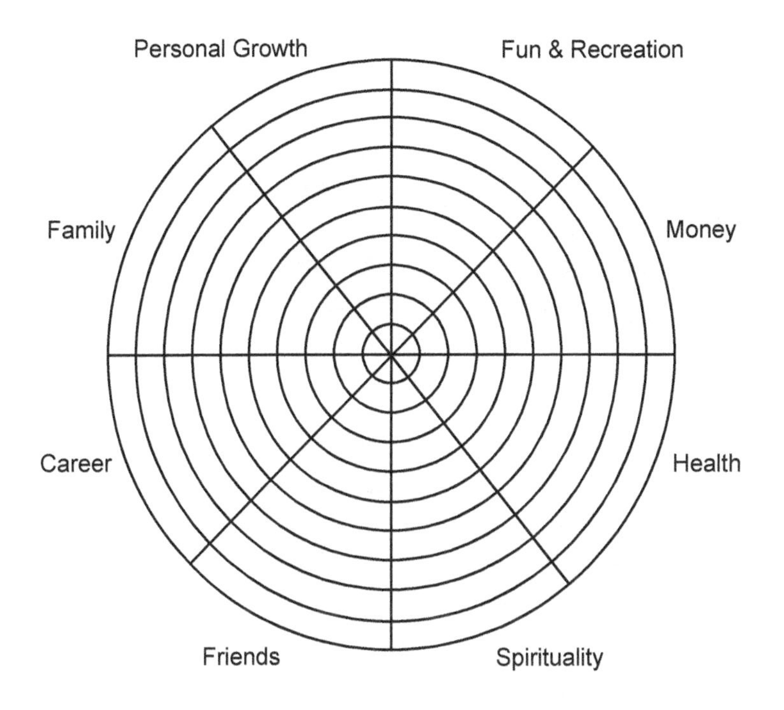
Personal Growth
Fun & Recreation
Family
Money
Career
Health
Friends
Spirituality

# Appendix 2

## Your Personal Values

This is a very comprehensive list. Begin by marking those values that most resonate with you in any of the categories. Taking those values, narrow it down again, repeating until you are able to bring it to your top 3. This is likely to be challenging – get ready to spend some time and energy as you identify your core values. These are your personal points of true north in which you try to live your life. Think about decisions you have made and which of these values guided you. Also, think about times when you disappointed yourself, where you were out of alignment. Those feelings are instructive because you likely were working against your values.

Your "core values" helps you along in life, to make the decisions that lead you to a life of greater happiness and fulfilment. As tempting as this is to skip over, try to stay with it until you have narrowed it down.

**Integrity**
Accountability
Candor
Commitment
Dependability
Dignity
Honesty
Honor
Responsibility
Sincerity
Transparency
Trust
Trustworthy
Truth

**Creativity**
Creation
Curiosity
Discovery
Exploration
Expressive
Imagination
Innovation
Inquisitive
Intuitive
Openness
Originality
Uniqueness
Wonder

**Presence**
Alertness
Attentive
Awareness
Beauty
Calm
Clear
Concentration
Focus
Silence
Simplicity
Solitude

**Intelligence**
Brilliance
Clever
Common sense
Decisiveness
Foresight
Genius
Insightful
Knowledge
Learning
Logic
Openness
Realistic
Reason
Reflective
Smart
Thoughtful
Understanding
Vision
Wisdom

**Strength**
Ambition
Assertiveness
Boldness
Confidence
Dedication
Discipline
Ferocious
Fortitude
Persistence
Power
Restraint
Rigor
Self-reliance
Temperance
Toughness
Vigor
Will

**Order**
Accuracy
Careful
Certainty
Cleanliness
Consistency
Control
Decisive
Economy
Justice
Lawful
Moderation
Organization
Security
Stability
Structure
Thorough
Timeliness

**Spirituality**
Adaptability
Altruism
Balance
Charity
Communication
Community
Connection
Consciousness
Contribution
Cooperation
Courtesy
Devotion
Equality
Ethical
Fairness
Family
Fidelity
Friendship
Generosity
Giving
Goodness
Harmony
Humility
Loyalty
Maturity
Meaning
Selfless
Sensitivity
Service
Sharing
Spirit
Stewardship
Support
Sustainability
Teamwork
Tolerance
Unity

**Achievement**
Accomplishment
Capable
Challenge
Challenge
Competence
Credibility
Determination
Development
Drive
Effectiveness
Empower
Endurance
Excellence
Famous
Greatness
Growth
Hard work
Improvement
Influence
Intensity
Leadership
Mastery
Motivation
Performance
Persistence
Potential
Power
Productivity
Professionalism
Prosperity
Recognition
Results-oriented

**Feelings**
Acceptance
Comfort
Compassion
Contentment
Empathy
Grace
Gratitude
Happiness
Hope
Inspiring
Irreverent
Joy
Kindness
Love
Optimism
Passion
Peace
Poise
Respect
Reverence
Satisfaction
Serenity
Thankful
Tranquility
Welcoming

**Freedom**
Independence
Individuality
Liberty

**Health**
Energy
Vitality

**Risk**
Significance
Skill
Skillfulness
Status
Success
Talent
Victory
Wealth
Winning

**Enjoyment**
Amusement
Enthusiasm
Experience
Fun
Playfulness
Recreation
Spontaneous
Surprise

**Courage**
Bravery
Conviction
Fearless
Valor

# Recommended Reading

Brown, Brene. The Gifts of Imperfection

Cain, Susan. Quiet: The Power of Introverts in a World That Can't Stop Talking

Cameron, Julia. The Artist's Way

Dickinson, Arlene. All In

Duckworth, Angela. Grit: The Power of Passion and Perseverance

Dweck, Carol. Mindset: The New Psychology of Success

Eurich, Tasha. Insight: How to Succeed by Seeing Yourself Clearly

Ferrucci, Piero. The Power of Kindness: The Unexpected benefits of Leading a Compassionate Life

Guillebeau, Chris. The Happiness of Pursuit

Hay, Louise. You Can Heal Your Life

Mate, Gabor. When the Body Says No

Obama, Michelle. Becoming

Rankin, Lissa. Mind Over Medicine.

Rubin, Gretchen. The Happiness Project

Sincero, Jen. You are a Badass

Van Der Kolk, Bessel. The Body Keeps the Score

# Notes

Pg. 37 Lereya ST1, Copeland WE2, Costello EJ2, Wolke D3. Adult mental health consequences of peer bullying and maltreatment in childhood: two cohorts in two countries. Lancet Journal of Psychiatry, 2015. Use granted via https://creativecommons.org/licenses/by/4.0/

Pg. 40 Robert Waldinger, What makes a good life, lessons from the longest study on happiness, Nov. 2015. To watch the full talk, visit TED.com

Pg. 60 AdmittingFailure.org "Fear, embarrassment, and intolerance of failure drives our learning underground and hinders innovation …." Used with permission from Ashley Good, Founder and CEO of Fail Forward, http://failforward.org

# Acknowledgements

This book wouldn't be complete if I missed taking the opportunity to thank the people who have left their mark on my heart and soul and helped me in my journey towards becoming the person capable of writing the book and seeing this project through.

First, to my brother Terry Boyle, from whom I always felt unconditional love and kindness. Life hasn't given us many chances to be together, but you gifted me with the knowledge that I mattered.

Next, my children Jack and Nicole, who have taught me as much as I hope I have taught you. Your individual impact in your chosen careers is my inspiration to dream big and continue to try and make a difference, one person at a time.

My cousin Lois Macpherson, for being there in one of the worst times of my life, opening your home and heart, even as you faced your own grief and loss. Thank you for your continued love and support as I venture forward on my Journey.

Psychotherapist Richard Lyke whose kindness and skill helped me heal and become a person capable of having functional and healthy relationships.

Friends are the family you choose, and I am fortunate to have a large chosen family who have helped me become the person I am today.

From every decade I have been blessed with friends who continue to give me support, love and are the role models for how I try to live my life. The list is long so by necessity I must abbreviate it to: Val Edwards, Jacquie Beavis, Colleen Colarelli, Cliff Beach, Beth Traynor and Jacqui Moraal.

Beth Watson, for believing in me as a writer before I did and for our fireside chats.

Sarah and Ryan O'Reilly – children of my heart and friends.

Each of you continue to inspire, encourage and support me, even though you are spread around the globe.

Patti Muldoon –Your unerring support and belief in my writing overall and in this project is immeasurable. I came to you for your technical expertise and found a friend. Thank you for all the ways you have improved my business and added to my personal life.

To my intrepid first draft readers- Monique Caissie, Merri McCartney, Jack Hickmott and Patti Muldoon. Your suggestions made the book better. Thank you.

My editor Keidi Keating for your guidance and helping me to stay out of the weeds and make this a more readable book.

And finally, to Jim Benoit, who has brought to this chapter of my life more love, more joy and more depth to who I am as a person. I am grateful beyond measure that when I was ready to embrace life fully, you arrived. I am blessed indeed.

Dear friends,

Thank you for adding this book to your library as you travel your own journey to joy. I hope it will give you encouragement and add to your knowledge as you continue your personal growth. If, after reading the book you have feedback, drop me a line or consider leaving a review on Amazon or GoodReads.

With gratitude,
*Frances Hickmott*

If you would like to hire Frances Hickmott as a keynote speaker at your next conference, as your transition mentor or are interested in signing up for a 100% event, please visit www.francesfound.com

CPSIA information can be obtained
at www.ICGtesting.com
Printed in the USA
LVHW090241071219
639763LV00003B/294/P